ARTICLES OF IMPEACHMENT AGAINST GEORGE W. BUSH

ARTICLES OF IMPEACHMENT AGAINST GEORGE W. BUSH

CENTER FOR CONSTITUTIONAL RIGHTS

MELVILLE HOUSE PUBLISHING
HOBOKEN, NEW JERSEY

BOOK DESIGN: DAVID KONOPKA

MELVILLE HOUSE PUBLISHING
300 OBSERVER HIGHWAY
THIRD FLOOR
HOBOKEN, NEW JERSEY 07030

WWW.MHPBOOKS.COM

SECOND EDITION MARCH 2006
A PAPERBACK ORIGINAL

ISBN: 1-933633-08-5

PRINTED IN THE UNITED STATES OF AMERICA

CONTENTS

INTRODUCTION

How can it be that we are yet again debating another presidential impeachment? Still weary from the Clinton impeachment battles and now completely exhausted from the momentous changes brought about by both 9/11 and this president—changes that include the Iraq war, indefinite detentions around the world, torture, domestic wiretapping, and more—we have all we can do to understand and perhaps resist some or all of these measures on an ad hoc basis. While any of the individual acts and policies outlined in the following articles would constitute an impeachable offense, taken as a whole, as a pattern and practice, they constitute something far more sinister, a plan to significantly weaken, if not destroy, our democracy.

As a consequence this nation is confronted with a grave constitutional crisis. We have a president staunchly committed to acquiring unprecedented amounts of power and using it in ways that conflict with the Constitution of the United States, international law, and the common understanding of morality. In short, although the president has sworn to uphold the Constitution, he is doing just the opposite. He is dismantling the Constitution of the United States. Primarily, his apparent purpose is to gather even more power—power unchecked by judicial or congressional scrutiny—to a presidency already bloated with power.

Simultaneously, summary arrests, in the United States and around the world, torture, indefinite detention, illegal surveillance, and suppression of free speech and protest have become commonplace. Yet worse, as all of this has happened the government has sought to eliminate any judicial oversight of its activities by weakening the judicial system in innumerable ways. The president has also disregarded Congress and thereby attempted to weaken its role. The consequence has been that the fundamental building block of American democracy, our system of separation of powers, has come under lethal attack.

How did it come about that we are in the constitutional crisis in which we find ourselves today? Before we discuss the reasons for this, or even the historical context, it seems useful to introduce some of the terminology and details that surround impeachment, the Constitution's nuclear option.

Article II, Section 4 of the Constitution provides that the president may be impeached for "Treason, Bribery, or other high Crimes and Misdemeanors." This was the mechanism that the framers of the Constitution provided Congress to protect itself from executive overreaching. Clearly the framers drafted this provision in the context of what they viewed as the history of their time, i.e., the conflict between the actions of the English king and the ideals of the English law. Thus, for the framers, impeachment was a key element of American democracy in that it provided an ultimate means to curtail abuses of, or unconstitutional expansion of, executive powers.

While bribery and treason were technically defined crimes that would inevitably subvert the Constitution, the more general and less defined concept of high crimes and misdemeanors was intended to identify that activity whereby the executive overstepped the bounds of public office or failed to faithfully execute the laws. Hamilton viewed it as an abuse or violation of the public trust. Thereby the framers provided a much more general category whereby the Constitution would also surely be subverted.

To place the present moment into the context of history, in 1868 President Andrew Johnson was acquitted by only one vote of the accusation of denying Congress its power. It was claimed that the president, unmindful of the oath that obliged him to faithfully execute the laws, denied that the legislation passed by Congress was either valid, or that he was required to comply.

President Clinton was impeached in 1999 for perjury and obstruction of justice. The circumstances of this impeachment, involving as they did, a personal affair, were unusual and are not applicable to the current situation. More pertinent, however, is the threatened impeachment and, ultimately, the resignation of Richard Nixon.

In 1974 President Nixon resigned before the House Judiciary Committee could vote on articles of impeachment. Those articles accused him of violating his constitutional oath 1) to faithfully execute the Office of the President; 2) to protect and defend the Constitution; and 3) to take care that the laws be faithfully executed. He did this by means of false and misleading statements, withholding information from Congress, condoning false statements, misuse of the CIA, and deceiving the people of the United States, as well, with false or misleading statements.

These are both the formal criteria and the precedents against which, when presented with the evidence, the reader may make a decision as to whether there is a valid basis for the impeachment of the current president.

Nine months after George W. Bush was sworn in as president, terrorists attacked the World Trade Center and murdered thousands. An active negligence of constitutional duties and boundaries commenced.

"You are either with us or you are with the terrorists," proclaimed the president. His attorney general, John Ashcroft, similarly declared:

"[T]o those who scare peace-loving people with phantoms of lost liberty; my message is this: Your tactics only aid terrorists—for they erode our national unity and diminish our resolve. They give ammunition to America's enemies, and pause to America's friends."

The message was clear: Opposition and dissent were treason and concern for constitutional rights was a technicality, a phantom that played into the hands of terrorism. Out of this antagonism to the Constitution that had long predated the attacks of 9/11 (as will be detailed) grew the full-blown attack on the system of checks and balances and the Bill of Rights that the following articles detail.

While these charges delineate a history for which one person, even the president of the United States, cannot be fully responsible and probably not even fully aware, this president was more than a willing accomplice to the severe damage to which our Constitution has been subjected. He has been an enthusiastic perpetrator of that damage. More importantly, when he swore to "preserve, protect, and defend" the Constitution, he should not have been merely mouthing words or repeating slogans. It is the thesis of this book that this promise must forever be embedded in the protoplasm of the man or woman who takes the oath. If it is not, we will all pay the price. If it is not, and if this oath is violated, the only just remedy is impeachment.

WILLIAM GOODMAN
Legal Director
Center for Constitutional Rights

ARTICLE I

George W. Bush, in his conduct of the Office of the President of the United States, has abused his power by violating the constitutional rights of citizens, impairing the due and proper administration of justice and the conduct of lawful inquiries, contravening the laws governing agencies of the executive branch, and failing to take care that the laws were faithfully executed by directing or authorizing the National Security Agency and various other agencies within the intelligence community to conduct electronic surveillance outside of the statutes Congress has prescribed as the exclusive means for such surveillance, and to use such information for purposes unknown but unrelated to any lawful function of his office; he has also concealed the existence of this unlawful program of electronic surveillance from Congress, the press, and the public. Wherefore George W. Bush, by such conduct, warrants impeachment and trial, and removal from office.

On December 17, 2005, George W. Bush admitted to the nation that, under his command, the National Security Agency (NSA) has for over four years engaged in a program of widespread warrantless electronic surveillance of telephone calls and emails. According to the administration, the Program targeted for surveillance only the communications of persons somehow affiliated with al Qaeda or organizations supportive of it. In some cases, the Program has targeted American citizens. Unnamed government sources have stated that approximately 500 persons inside the United States and 5,000 outside of the United States have been targets. According to the government, the Program only intercepted communications where one party was thought to be located outside the United States (although in many instances purely domestic communications were intercepted). However, media reports have indicated that the interceptions themselves took place inside the United States—by plugging into large phone companies' switching systems located in New York and other places in the United States where international calls enter the country through transoceanic fiber optic cables.

This program of warrantless electronic surveillance is clearly illegal. To the extent that electronic surveillance is essential to protect the national security of this country, Congress has provided a comprehensive set of procedures for such surveillance in the Foreign Intelligence Surveillance Act (FISA), which allows for court authorization of such surveillance only when the government produces evidence that the individual who is a target is an agent of a foreign power or foreign terrorist group. FISA includes provisions allowing for retroactive approval of surveillance up to 72 hours after it has begun in emergency situations, and for warrantless surveillance during the first fifteen days of a war. Congress has mandated that FISA and specified provisions of the criminal code shall be the "*exclusive* means by which electronic surveillance… may be conducted" (emphasis added). Yet the president declined to pursue these "exclusive means," and instead unilaterally and secretly authorized electronic surveillance without judicial approval or Congressional authorization.

The facts (among others) that interceptions were made within the U.S. and that U.S. citizens were surveilled places at least some of the NSA Program squarely within the area regulated by FISA. The fact that surveillance under the Program took place with no review of its reasonableness by the FISA Court (or any other court) makes it clearly criminal under FISA. The law is absolutely clear in this regard, but the facts present a number of open questions: Who was the administration actually targeting, and what was its motive in circumventing FISA? Because impeachment of an elected official is a grave act that undoes the democratically-expressed will of voters, it is generally believed that presidential misconduct must present a threat to the democratic system of government or an egregious abuse of power before it will constitute an impeachable offense. Whether the president broke the law in good faith while pursuing the best interests of the country or for his own political ends is therefore a central question to consider in deciding whether the NSA surveillance program warrants impeachment. However, because so little is known about these motives—who was the administration spying on with the Program, and why?—the question of whether it was impeachable conduct requires us to examine a number of different factual contingencies. In order to analyze whether this still-secretive conduct constitutes an impeachable offense requires going into the legal and factual background in some detail.

The Fourth Amendment states that:

> The right of the people to be secure in their persons, houses, papers, and effects, against unreasonable searches and seizures, shall not be violated, and no Warrants shall issue, but upon probable cause, supported by Oath or affirmation, and particularly describing the place to be searched, and the persons or things to be seized.

Although on its face the literal language of the amendment only prohibits "unreasonable searches and seizures," the Supreme Court has consistently held that searches without a warrant are presumptively unreasonable, so that, except in a limited number of exceptional circumstances, warrantless searches are unconstitutional. The Fourth Amendment requires the government to show probable cause—that is, evidence supporting the conclusion that the target of the search is involved in criminal activity—before a judge may issue a warrant. Moreover, all warrants must meet the "particularity" requirement: They must describe specifically what the government is looking for. Unreasonable searches that violate the Fourth Amendment will support civil damages actions against the perpetrators, and any evidence seized in violation of the Fourth Amendment (and all evidence subsequently found through the use of such tainted evidence) must be excluded from use in any subsequent criminal proceedings.

For the first 90 years of the telephone's existence, it was thought that electronic surveillance of phone conversations stood outside the protections of the Fourth Amendment as long as there was no physical trespass involved in the interception of the communications. (So, breaking into a suspect's house to install a bug might implicate the Fourth Amendment, but a bug planted in a public phone booth, or a wiretap installed in telephone company circuits, would not.) The Supreme Court changed this in *Katz v. United States* (1967), overruling *Olmstead v. United States* (1928) and holding that because the target of the surveillance had an "expectation of privacy" in the phone conversations at issue (held within a closed public telephone booth), those conversations were protected by the Fourth Amendment. (In so holding, the court famously stated "the Fourth Amendment protects people, not places.")

The question of what kind of warrant would be appropriate for phone taps was thus raised for the first time in the wake of the *Katz* decision. Earlier that year, the Supreme Court had suggested in *Berger v. New York* (1967) that interception of in-transit communications in real time raised special concerns: Whereas the "particularity" requirement of the Fourth Amendment's Warrants Clause places limits on places to be searched and physical objects to be seized, by nature it is difficult to limit the information seized while eavesdropping in a similar way. A warrant directed at a particular phone line or even at one particular person's phone conversations would sweep in conversations with any number of other persons on all matter of subjects. In response to *Berger* and *Katz*, Congress passed the 1968 Wiretap Act (aka Title III of the Omnibus Crime Control and Safe Streets Act), which requires not just a warrant but a "super-warrant"—a so-called Title III Order—to allow law enforcement access to the protected communications at issue. Its requirements are higher than those for ordinary search warrants: The government must show in its affidavits why normal investigative procedures have not succeeded in obtaining the required evidence, any warrant-order must set forth procedures to minimize intrusiveness on privacy, and so forth.

Congress reacted to the court's decisions quickly, responding with thorough, thoughtful legislation throughout this period. However, as of 1968 the court had still said nothing about surveillance on foreign powers; the prevailing thinking was that the president had some implied power to eavesdrop on communications with a foreign power or its agents in carrying out his duty to protect the national security. Indeed, the original Wiretap Act of 1968 contained the following text:

Nothing contained in this chapter [the Wiretap Act]... shall limit the constitutional power of the President to take such measures as he deems necessary to protect the Nation against actual or potential attack or other hostile acts of a foreign power, to obtain foreign intelligence information deemed essential to the security of the United States.... Nor shall anything contained in this chapter be deemed to limit the constitutional power of the President to take such measures as he deems necessary to protect the United States against the overthrow of the Government by force or other unlawful means, or against any other clear and present danger to the structure or existence of the Government. (1968)

This was eventually removed by FISA in 1978.

In the landmark case *United States v. United States District Court* (*Keith*) (1972) the Supreme Court held that domestic surveillance for national security purposes was subject to the restrictions of the Fourth Amendment. In *Keith*, purely domestic groups stood accused of bombing CIA offices. Warrantless wiretaps had been carried out on the defendants. The government argued a national security-based intelligence-gathering exemption from the warrant requirement. The Supreme Court rejected the argument, holding that the Fourth Amendment required "prior judicial approval" for the wiretaps in the case at hand—which the government claimed were directed at "attempts of domestic organizations to attack and subvert the existing structure of government" but where there was no allegation "of any involvement, directly or indirectly, of a foreign power."

Just as *Katz* had left open questions that Congress resolved with Title III, the *Keith* Court left to Congress the task of setting forth "reasonable standards" for issuance of such "national security" warrants. In response, Congress again acted, passing the Foreign Intelligence Surveillance Act (FISA) in 1978. However, in the intervening period, widespread spying on American citizens by various federal law enforcement and intelligence agencies, including the NSA, became public. A committee led by Senator Frank Church produced vast reports on the scope of this surveillance, showing that political activists including Dr. Martin Luther King were targets. Congress was split between members who sought to limit presidential power and those who believed the executive should have nearly unlimited power to carry out such surveillance. The statute that resulted from this debate was a compromise between the two extremes, but a compromise intended to control essentially all surveillance involving a domestic target or an interception on U.S. soil.

FISA provides a comprehensive statutory scheme for conducting electronic surveillance for foreign intelligence or national security purposes. FISA requires that all such surveillance (with narrow exceptions) be conducted pursuant to orders from the statutorily created Foreign Intelligence Surveillance Court.

"Electronic surveillance" is defined by FISA at 50 U.S.C. § 1801(f). The definition includes the acquisition of any communication carried by a common carrier via wire or cable if acquired by a surveillance device in the United States. The definition also includes acquisition of certain wire or radio communications sent to or from a United States person that are acquired by targeting that United States person, acquisition of certain radio communications (which might include, for example, the signals sent from a cell phone tower to a cell phone), and installation or use of any surveillance device, even those not used to intercept wire or radio communications, in certain circumstances.

FISA's definitions of "foreign power" and "agent of a foreign power" are broad and inclusive. "Foreign power" includes not only foreign governments, factions thereof, and entities openly directed and controlled by foreign governments, but also any "group engaged in international terrorism or activities in preparation therefor," any "foreign-based political organization, not substantially composed of United States persons," or any "entity that is directed and controlled by a foreign government or governments." "Agent of a foreign power" is defined to include any person (whether a United States person or not) who carries out clandestine intelligence activities for a foreign power, engages in sabotage or terrorism, or who enters the United States under a false identity on behalf of a foreign power or assumes such an identity while in the United States. The definition also includes non-United States persons who act as officers or employees of a "foreign power," who conspire to or do aid, abet, or carry out clandestine intelligence activities in the United States, or who carry out terrorism or "activities in preparation" for terrorism. In short, the FISA statute covers a broad array of potential surveillance targets.

Electronic surveillance orders requested by the government pursuant to FISA § 1802(b) are rarely rejected. The Foreign Intelligence Surveillance Court rejected not a single one of the thousands of requests for surveillance orders it received from its creation in 1979 through 2002. From 1995 through 2004 the Court received 10,617 such requests and turned down four.

These statistics are unsurprising given the composition of the court and the standards it is called on to apply. Judges on the court are appointed to temporary terms—whereas they are all life-tenured federal district court judges, they serve seven year terms on the Foreign Intelligence Surveillance Court while they continue their regular duties as federal judges. They are appointed not by elected officials (federal judges, in contrast, are named by the president and confirmed by the Senate) but by the chief justice, who need not answer to voters. Constitutional challenges to FISA on these grounds in the lower federal courts have generally failed.

FISA also allows for retroactive approval of warrantless electronic surveillance in emergency situations. In order to carry out such surveillance, the attorney general must first determine that the factual basis for a FISA order exists, but that "an emergency situation" requires the surveillance to be put into effect before a court order can be sought. Retrospective approval from the Foreign Intelligence Surveillance Court must be sought as soon as practicable, but in no event later than 72 hours after the attorney general authorizes the surveillance. (Congress extended this time period from 24 to 72 hours by statute passed on December 28, 2001.)

In addition to providing a warrant procedure allowing for the issuance of orders by the Foreign Intelligence Surveillance Court authorizing national security electronic surveillance, Congress delineated in FISA sections 1802(a) and 1811 the only exceptions under which the president might conduct such electronic surveillance without some form of judicial warrant.

FISA § 1802(a) authorizes warrantless electronic surveillance in certain limited circumstances, primarily involving communications between and among foreign governments, factions thereof, and/or entities openly directed and controlled by foreign governments, where "there is no substantial likelihood that the surveillance will acquire the contents of any communication to which a United States person is a party." (The same section also allows surveillance of foreign embassies located within the United States.)

FISA § 1811 also allows the president to authorize warrantless electronic surveillance for fifteen days following a formal declaration of war by Congress. The legislative history of this section shows it was designed to give Congress enough time (roughly two weeks) to pass any modifications to the wiretap laws necessitated by the state of war. Rather than giving the president carte blanche during declared wars, this 15 day exemption was designed to ensure that Congress had a say concerning all surveillance practices, and had time to formulate a reasoned opinion as to the balance to be struck between flexibility for law enforcement and oversight mechanisms, even in wartime.

FISA sections 1802(a) and 1811 are the only provisions of FISA allowing for warrantless electronic surveillance without subsequent, retroactive judicial approval. To emphasize this point, FISA eliminated the reservation clause originally placed in the U.S. Code by the 1968 Wiretap Act, former 18 U.S.C. § 2511(3) (1968), which stated "[n]othing contained in this [Act]...shall limit the constitutional power of the President" to carry out national security surveillance. By establishing this comprehensive scheme of regulation, Congress indicated its intent to preclude any implied presidential powers in the area occupied by FISA. And to make the point completely clear, Congress provided that FISA and specified provisions of the criminal code would be the "*exclusive* means by which electronic surveillance...and the interception of domestic wire, oral, and electronic communications may be conducted" (emphasis added).

Congress further established (in 50 USC § 1809) that conducting electronic surveillance without such statutory authorization is a felony.

SPECIFICATION FIRST. The NSA Program is flatly criminal. The administration has made admissions about how the existing program works that show that the Program is flatly illegal under FISA. For example, administration officials have admitted that United States citizens were targeted by the program. Officials have told members of the media that the interceptions took place on United States soil, and that at least one party to the calls and emails is a person within the United States. All of this places the Program within the definition of "electronic surveillance" in FISA, meaning that FISA governs the surveillance. Even when the targets are "agents of foreign powers," the administration would have to seek an order from the FISA court—a retroactive order in emergencies—in order to conduct the surveillance lawfully, absent any declaration of war.

Without such a court order, the Program violates FISA, and officials who engaged in surveillance, or used or disclosed information gathered by the Program knowing the information was gathered without statutory authorization, have committed a felony. (Note that the media has reported that the NSA shared surveillance results from the Program with other agencies—including the Defense Intelligence Agency, Department of Homeland Security, FBI, and CIA. Two government sources told reporter James Risen that some 10 to 20 percent of FISA orders issued by the court today are obtained through the use of information disclosed to law enforcement agencies by the NSA. One judge of the FISA Court (James Robertson) reportedly resigned in protest over the fact that illegally obtained information had been used to induce him to issue FISA surveillance orders.) Here there was no such review by any court, or indeed by anyone outside the executive branch—or even outside the NSA, for officials have stated that NSA staff employees have complete autonomy to pick out targets, with oversight only from their shift supervisors. These criminal violations are clearly ongoing: The president has stated that he intends to reauthorize the program "for as long as our nation faces a continuing threat from al Qaeda and related groups."

SPECIFICATION SECOND. The classical, strict view of Congress's impeachment authority has been that abuse of presidential power is impeachable only when it endangers the nation as a polity. To be an impeachable offense, an abuse—even a violation of law—must itself severely threaten the system of government or constitute a grievous abuse of official power, or both. This high standard was met in the surveillance charges brought against President Richard Nixon.

Article 2 of the Nixon impeachment articles dealt with Abuse of Power. Nixon was charged with "repeatedly engag[ing] in conduct violating the constitutional rights of citizens, impairing the due and proper administration of justice and the conduct of lawful inquiries, or contravening the laws governing agencies of the executive branch and the purposes of these agencies." Specifically, the House charged President Nixon with misusing the intelligence services by directing or allowing them "to conduct or continue electronic surveillance or other investigations for purposes unrelated to national security, the enforcement of laws, or any other lawful function of his office." Clearly, such surveillance met the standard of endangering the polity and the system of government—in the House's words, Nixon's actions were "subversive of constitutional government, to the great prejudice of the cause of law and justice and to the manifest injury of the people of the United States."

On this strict view of impeachable offenses, President Bush's motivation for carrying out the NSA warrantless surveillance program is crucial, and here we know little directly about it. Just like a jury trying to measure the intent of a criminal defendant, we are forced to evaluate the president's motivations here by indirect evidence. In assessing the motivation of the president and other administration officials, we need to rely on facts leaked to the press, circumstances, and from the few times administration officials have directly discussed their motivations in creating the program. The best starting point in this difficult endeavor is this last category—the defenses the administration has offered for the program—for we do know that much of what officials have said about their motives is implausible.

To begin with, the primary defense offered by the administration has been that the Program allows it to put wiretaps into place with unparalleled speed, far faster than FISA procedures would allow. However, this explanation—the primary defense offered by the attorney general in his first press conference on the Program—is disingenuous. FISA allows the government to put surveillance in place first, and go to the court afterwards—within 72 hours—in emergencies. There is nothing faster than a retroactive warrant. The administration has claimed that the government needs to take time to carefully review the factual basis for such wiretaps before even using the emergency procedures, lest the court reject the application after the fact. This concern is also disingenuous, because the FISA Court almost never denies wiretap orders, as noted above.

The president and his subordinates have also consistently argued that they believed that Congress had implicitly authorized this surveillance when it passed the authorization to use military force in Afghanistan (the so-called AUMF) in 2001. However, Congress made slight adjustments to the wiretapping statutes in December 2001 (extending the period for retroactive approval of wiretaps from 24 to 72 hours), just a few weeks after passing the AUMF. Congress would not have needed to do so if it intended to authorize wholesale unchecked surveillance with the AUMF. It is likely that the administration actually believed Congress was unlikely to approve of the NSA Program. In his December 19, 2005, press briefing, Attorney General Gonzales said the administration thought about asking Congress for approval of changes to the FISA statute to make the NSA program legal, but they did not ask Congress for permission because they thought Congress would not grant it. It is disingenuous for the administration to say, on the one hand, that Congress *implicitly* approved the NSA Program while also saying that it thought Congress would not have approved of it *explicitly.*

Related to this claim is the notion that the president had authority to create the Program because presidents have an inherent constitutional power to conduct warrantless surveillance to gather foreign intelligence. This argument ignores the fact that Congress has legislated in the area by passing FISA in 1978. The federal appellate court cases the administration cites for this principle are all cases decided under the standards applicable *before* Congress created FISA (*United States v. Clay*, *United States v. Brown*, *United States v. Butenko*, *United States v. Buck*; and *United States v. Truong* (a 1980 opinion dealing with surveillance that ended in January 1978, prior to the October 1978 passage of FISA, and thus applying pre-FISA standards)). So are the historical precedents the administration has offered in its defense: President Lincoln's telegraph wiretaps during the civil war, President Wilson's wiretaps in World War I, President Franklin D. Roosevelt's wiretaps during World War II. FISA was intended to be comprehensive, covering all electronic surveillance of foreign powers and their agents, and FISA makes all surveillance outside its terms a felony, including the NSA program.

The only way the administration could claim FISA does not apply is to challenge the power of Congress to create any such restriction on the president's information gathering powers—essentially to argue that the president has inherent powers in this area that Congress lacks any authority to limit. That extreme argument has never been adopted by any court and is contrary to decades of precedents holding that powers not expressly assigned by the Constitution are shared between the executive and legislative branches and thus subject to legislative regulation. (The administration has argued, in its supplemental brief in *In re Sealed Case*, 02-001 [For. Intell. Surveillance Ct. of Review, Sept. 25, 2002], Part III.A, that the "primary purpose" test successfully challenged in that case would unconstitutionally trench on the president's inherent intelligence gathering function.)

Occasionally officials have argued that the "probable cause" standard that must be met to issue a FISA wiretap order is too burdensome, and that, instead, the government should be able to proceed under a lesser "reasonable suspicion" standard. FISA does not require probable cause that a surveillance target has participated in a crime; it only requires probable cause that a target is an agent of certain types of foreign political or terrorist organizations. The administration has claimed that only individuals with some link to al Qaeda have been the targets of the program; if there was indeed some evidence linking a person to al Qaeda, the government could have easily obtained lawful orders from the FISA court to conduct the surveillance. Again, the diminished form of "probable cause" required by the FISA statute has never been a hard standard for the government to meet in practice, as the FISA Court has approved most of the applications put forth by the government.

However, even if it had a basis in practical reality, the "probable cause" standard is unlikely to have been the administration's true motive in pursuing the Program. In June 2002, Republican Senator Michael DeWine of Ohio introduced a bill (S.2659) that would "modify the standard of proof for issuance of [FISA] orders...from probable cause to reasonable suspicion." The Justice Department said in a position statement that "the Administration at this time is not prepared to support" the DeWine amendment. The Justice Department refused to support the amendment because it had no evidence that FISA was hindering its efforts to get the warrants it needed, and because it feared that such wiretaps might violate the Fourth Amendment and thus jeopardize any prosecutions based on such tainted evidence. The administration could have asked Congress to modify FISA at any time if it genuinely believed the statute was standing in the way of counterterrorism operations. But it never did.

The president has argued that he could not safely have gone to Congress asking for approval of the specific forms of surveillance carried out by the NSA because terrorists will react to the disclosures about the program made in the course of legislative debate—"The enemy will think 'Here's what they do—adjust,'" as the president put it. Of course, this argument is facially disingenuous: Terrorists already know the government is trying to listen in on their communications—the hijackers took elaborate precautions against surveillance even before 9/11, when the nation was not yet on permanent alert. And it makes no difference to al Qaeda members whether they are being wiretapped with a warrant or without a warrant.

Finally, one might question whether the president was effectively insulated from the illegality of the Program by the fact that he relied on the advice of his subordinates and particularly his legal counsel. Regardless of what happens in the investigation of the program, we may never know what legal advice the president received concerning the legality of the Program, given the fact that that advice may be subject to multiple privileges. However, media reports indicate that many high-level officials within the administration felt this program was illegal. It has been widely reported that Deputy Attorney General James Comey refused to sign off on a periodic reauthorization of the Program in March 2004, when John Ashcroft was in the hospital, and White House officials were forced to visit Ashcroft in his hospital bed to seek reapproval. Ashcroft reportedly was himself reluctant to sign the reauthorization at that time. It has also been reported that the chief judge of the FISA Court, Colleen Kollar-Kotelly, raised doubts about the legality of the Program when she was briefed about it after she became chief judge in 2003, and that these concerns lead to the temporary suspension of the Program at that time.

SPECIFICATION THIRD. All of the justifications for the program offered by the administration are flimsy—"strained and unrealistic" in the words of Republican Senator Arlen Specter—but they leave a void when we turn to the question of what the actual motivation behind the Program might have been.

One possible explanation concerns the scope of the Program. If the Program is in fact as broad as the newspapers have reported—if it involved data-mining of the sort that requires the government to listen to virtually every international phone call with the help of voice-recognition software—then it is so far outside any sort of surveillance ever attempted by an American government before that it would be impossible to adapt judicial oversight to manage it. The warrant process is predicated on the idea that the "things" (here, the communications) to be "searched" (here, eavesdropped upon) will be limited in some way—that they will be described with "particularity" in the written warrant the court issues, both so that that written document can serve as a guide to the officers carrying out the search, and to guarantee that the warrant that issues will have some relation to the underlying evidence establishing probable cause. As the Supreme Court noted in *Berger v. New York*, these ideas are difficult to translate into the context of wiretap orders, but that is simply grounds for being more careful to limit the nature of wiretap orders, and over the last four decades Congress has generally required that all wiretap orders utilize "minimization procedures" and other safeguards described above to reduce the intrusiveness of this inherently open-ended form of surveillance.

However, a data-mining program where the government scanned the contents of every international email and phone call for individual words or patterns of activity would be so inherently incompatible with such safeguards that it would be impossible to run if any such requirements applied to it. Since the program became public, government officials have denied that any such "data mining" aspect to the program exists, but the current firestorm is not the first time such a program has been attributed to this administration: John Poindexter's "Total Information Awareness" (TIA) program (disclosed to the public in 2002) also sought to gather together information from diverse sources ranging from public consumer databases to covert surveillance (using speech recognition technology), and to collect this information into a master database on all of society for the use of the intelligence agencies and law enforcement. Nixon adviser John Dean stated that, "Bush may have outdone Nixon" due to the scope of the surveillance reportedly subsumed by the NSA Program; in its data-mining aspect, it could have effectively included everyone in our society, not just (as in Nixon's case) the president's political opponents.

Another possible explanation turns on this administration's long-term agenda for advancing executive power. Clearly the administration wanted to avoid having to be accountable to any court—even one as friendly to the administration as the FISA Court—in the day-to-day operation of the Program. The administration also clearly wanted to avoid any accountability to Congress, by ignoring the FISA statue even when Congress clearly intended for that statute to be the "exclusive means" for carrying out such surveillance, and made all surveillance outside of FISA and the Wiretap Act a felony. The president did so even though Congress has generally granted his administration all the additional surveillance powers it has requested in the years since 9/11. Given the general ease with which the other branches have acquiesced to the president's demands in the past, perhaps the only explanation for the NSA Program that makes sense is that this administration wants to establish that it is not bound by the law at all—that the Program is part of a general effort to reverse what Vice President Cheney called the "erosion of presidential power" after the Watergate era.

One last explanation turns on the nature of the communications targeted by the Program. It is possible that the NSA is engaging in surveillance that even FISA judges would never approve of: conversations of attorneys and their clients, or of journalists with their sources. It is possible that the Program was at least partially motivated by the desire to make it more difficult for plaintiffs abroad to successfully litigate challenges to this administration's detention and interrogation tactics in the "war on terror."

If any of these motivations turns out to have underlain the NSA Program, the president's action in authorizing the Program might meet the criteria for "high Crimes and Misdemeanors" on even the strictest legal definition of what constitutes an impeachable offense. A Total Information Awareness-style program would clearly be subversive of constitutional government and democracy by nature of its scope. The notion of systematically attacking the separation of powers for no substantive purpose other than the advancement of executive power is also potentially subversive of the constitutional structure the president swore in his oath of office to uphold. And if the Program sought to eavesdrop upon attorney-client communications with the knowledge that this would subvert legal process in court challenges to administration policy, or upon journalist-source communications with the knowledge that this could subvert negative media coverage of the administration, this is an obvious abrogation of the president's obligation to uphold the law and therefore obviously impeachable by anyone's standard.

Finally, it is worth noting that the president has gone to great lengths to conceal the existence of the Program from the public. Apparently the president met with editors from *The New York Times* in an effort to stop them from publishing the story disclosing the existence of the Program in December of 2005. Certainly, this sort of cover-up of illegal (indeed, criminal) administration activity is subversive of the democratic process.

SPECIFICATION FOURTH. The president's misconduct in authorizing the Program is itself potentially a felony under FISA and certainly has led others following his commands to commit criminal violations of FISA. Does the mere fact that this conduct is a felony make it impeachable conduct, regardless of whether it was otherwise subversive of constitutional government and a general abuse of government trust power?

Here, much depends not on the nature of the Program or the president's motivations in implementing it, but on legal theories concerning the limits of the impeachment power. The president is thought to have immunity from criminal prosecutions while in office—that is, while the president can be indicted by state or federal authorities, he need not stand trial on any charges until after his term (or terms) of office have expired. This immunity stems from separation of powers concerns. The president is a branch of government unto himself (unlike the 535 members of Congress or the nine Supreme Court justices and hundreds of lower federal judges), and therefore it would negate the votes of Americans to disable him from carrying out his office by forcing him to defend against criminal charges during his term of office. Similarly, by making the president face charges while in office, the other branches could effectively imprison the president, leaving no one responsible for administering laws passed by Congress—and thus removing an important check on the power of Congress. (To cite just one example, the president is responsible for deciding which of the many criminal laws passed by Congress to give enforcement priority to in a world of limited law enforcement and prosecutorial resources. Where the presidency is weakened by impeachment, the office is less likely to be a strong counterweight to Congressional priorities in this regard.)

Therefore, it has generally been believed that the president must be impeached first—and thereby removed from office—before being forced to face criminal charges against him.

This immunity may cut both ways, however. If the criminal charges are considered significant enough that the president ought to be forced to face them in a timely fashion, then perhaps impeachment is a mere preliminary to criminal prosecution—a formality designed to ensure that an effective executive branch can continue during the criminal trial. On the other hand, such an impeachment would negate the votes of Americans. (Of course, the fact that the president may have pressured newspapers to delay reporting the story until after the 2004 election might play into the weight accorded to this last factor.) To some extent, this kind of formalistic thinking underlay the impeachment of President Clinton.

Of course, if purely private misconduct—without further implications for the integrity of government or the trust of the American people beyond its mere illegality—can constitute "high Crimes and Misdemeanors," then the blatant illegality of the NSA Program may be sufficient to render President Bush impeachable. On such an interpretation of the impeachment power, the president's intent may not matter—the fact that he committed *criminal* misconduct may be enough in itself.

ARTICLE II

The impeachment of George W. Bush, President of the United States, is warranted by his initiation and continuation of the Iraq war. The initiation and continuation of the war constitutes a high crime and misdemeanor and is illegal as well. In undertaking that war, George W. Bush violated his oath of office and constitutional obligation that the laws be faithfully executed.

George W. Bush has subverted the Constitution, its guarantee of a republican form of government, and the constitutional separation of powers by undermining the rightful authority of Congress to declare war, oversee foreign affairs, and make appropriations. He did so by justifying the war with false and misleading statements and deceived the people of the United States as well as Congress. He denied the electorate the right to make an informed choice and thereby undermined democracy.

George W. Bush also committed fraud against the United States by lying to and intentionally misleading Congress about the reasons for the Iraq war.

George W. Bush acted contrary to his trust as president, and subverted the constitutional government to the prejudice of law and justice and the manifest injury of the people of the United States. Wherefore George W. Bush, by such conduct, warrants impeachment and trial, and removal from office.

The means used to implement this course of conduct or plan included the following:

SPECIFICATION FIRST. The president failed in his oath and constitutional obligation that the laws be faithfully executed. The laws of the United States include the United Nations Charter. The Charter is a treaty of the United States signed by the president and ratified by the Senate. The Charter prohibits war against another country except as authorized by the Security Council, or in self-defense. The laws regulating the use of armed force or war also include laws that emerged from the Nuremberg trials in Germany when Nazi war criminals were tried for making aggressive war; such a war is called a "crime against peace." It is considered to be the most serious international crime. A crime against peace is a war that is not authorized by the United Nations or undertaken in self-defense. Self-defense is defined by the UN Charter as the employment of force against an "armed attack." It also includes anticipatory self-defense. A country need not await an actual attack to use self-defense; if it is to be imminently attacked it can try and prevent that attack with force. This is sometimes referred to as "preemptive attack." However, the concept of self-defense does not include a preventive attack. In other words, one country cannot attack another just because at some time in the future it believes the other country might launch an attack.

In attacking Iraq the Bush administration claimed it had the right to make a preemptive attack on Iraq, but the administration did not show that Iraq posed an "immediate threat" or that it was planning an "imminent attack." Therefore an attack on Iraq could not be legal under the doctrine of self-defense. While there were many Security Council resolutions regarding Iraq, and many claims that Iraq violated those resolutions, there was never a Security Council resolution authorizing the use of force against Iraq. That would have been the only lawful basis for the U.S. to attack Iraq. The war against Iraq cannot be justified as a measure of self-defense, nor did it have Security Council approval. Thus, in going to war, President Bush committed an international crime, a "crime against peace," and failed to execute the laws of the United States.

President Bush's claim that he could justify an attack against Iraq without UN approval even if it was not in self-defense is an illegal policy for which President Bush and members of his administration have been laying the groundwork for a number of years. Prior to 9/11, members of the Bush administration had been putting forth a new paradigm for use of the American military. Senior administration officials Dick Cheney, Paul Wolfowitz, and Colin Powell had argued in 1992, in the Pentagon's "Defense Planning Guidance" document, that the U.S. could not allow any rival force to gain power, including any regional force, and that the military force of the United States could be used "preemptively." By "preemptively" the document meant: without there being any immediate threat to the United States. Even before the Bush administration took office, future members of the administration had plans to invade Iraq and remove Saddam Hussein. For example, in December 1997, Paul Wolfowitz was involved in writing a guide called "Saddam Must Go: A How-To Guide"; in May 1999, when a candidate, Bush discussed invading Iraq if he were elected; just prior to the election, a conservative think tank called Project for a New American Century, whose membership at the time included Paul Wolfowitz and Donald Rumsfeld, stated that one of the goals of American foreign policy should be to build up a U.S. presence in the Persian Gulf and get rid of Saddam Hussein, but in order to do so and get away with it a government would need "some catastrophic and catalyzing event—like a new Pearl Harbor." There are numerous similar instances. Considering this history, it can be proven that administration officials, in advance of elected office or appointment, were planning to use force outside of the prohibitions contained in law and had plans to invade Iraq.

Subsequent to the attacks of 9/11, President Bush and the administration put into place their policy of preemptive war, a policy that is completely unlawful. President Bush and these officials also saw and used the attacks of 9/11 as the "Pearl Harbor" needed to justify the invasion of Iraq; the attacks of 9/11 could be used as a cover to give the invasion a legal justification. This was so even though there was no evidence Iraq had any involvement with 9/11. On September 25, 2001, a Justice Department memo approved the legality of preemptive war. Like the other memos issued from the Justice Department that approved torture and warrantless wiretapping, this memo did not reach the threshold of legality; it was simply a way for the president to cover the obvious illegality of his actions.

In President Bush's State of the Union address on January 29, 2002, the president articulated the doctrine of preemptive war, stating that the United States will "not wait on events while dangers gather." In that speech he also called Iraq a "grave and growing danger," and deemed it part of the "Axis of Evil." This was all a way of preparing the American people and Congress to accept an illegal war against Iraq. The president continued on this propaganda offensive, arguing for the necessity of preemptive strikes in a speech he gave in June 2002 at West Point. President Bush declared that the United States could use military force against any state it perceives to be hostile, or that seeks to acquire biological, chemical, or nuclear weapons, or is viewed as aiding terrorism: "And our security will require all Americans to be forward looking and resolute, to be ready for preemptive action when necessary to defend our liberty and our lives."

As stated above, this doctrine of preventive or preemptive attack on another nation has absolutely no support in law, and yet it became the doctrine under which the United States attacked Iraq. Under our Constitution, the UN Charter is the supreme law of the land; its prohibition on aggression is fundamental. The president failed to heed its command. Thus, President Bush is impeachable for his failure to execute the laws of the United States.

SPECIFICATION SECOND. As stated, even prior to Bush's presidency, Bush and his administration had plans to invade Iraq and overthrow Saddam Hussein. However, the president and his administration needed to find a justification for such an invasion for the purposes of obtaining Congressional approval. Under the United States Constitution, it is the Congress that decides when the nation goes to war, and it is the Congress that appropriates money for any war. From the time the current administration took office until the present, President Bush and his administration engaged in fraud and conspiracy to obtain Congressional consent, as well as the support of the American people, by justifying the war with false and misleading statements, the withholding of information, and intentionally misleading Congress and the American people about the reasons for the war. The administration did so with hundreds of misleading statements and lies, told through the media, at various speeches, and to Congress itself. In March 2004, the Democratic staff of the House Committee on Governmental Reform concluded that five leading administration officials of the Bush administration made hundreds of misleading statements about the threat posed by Iraq. In 125 public appearances, the staff documented 237 misleading statements. Today, more than half of Americans believe the Bush administration deliberately misled the public about the reasons for the war with Iraq. This intentional effort to mislead Congress and the American people constitutes grounds for impeachment. It undercut the ability of Congress to decide when to go to war, constituted a fraud on the United States, and undercut the rights of Americans to make the kind of informed choice that is necessary in a constitutional democracy. There are hundreds of examples that have been detailed in the media and in the halls of Congress. Set forth below is some of this history that amply supports impeachment.

The administration based its case on two false propositions: first, that Saddam Hussein supported al Qaeda and Osama bin Laden, and was involved in the attacks on 9/11; second, that the Iraqi government either had or was in the process of developing nuclear, chemical, or biological weapons of mass destruction (WMDs). None of this was true, and the administration knew it. Their interest in using 9/11 as cover for attacking Iraq was evident within hours of 9/11. On the very day of the 9/11 attacks, Defense Secretary Rumsfeld instructed his aides to start thinking about attacking Iraq. The day after the attacks, Rumsfeld said that Iraq had better targets for military action than Afghanistan, implying that we should attack Iraq even if it had nothing to do with 9/11, and Cheney claimed Iraq was allied with al Qaeda. The theme that Iraq was allied with al Qaeda was to be one of the dominant motifs of the Bush administration through the time Iraq was attacked, although the evidence for such an alliance was non-existent. On September 15, 2001, Bush stated that "once Afghanistan has been dealt with, it will be Iraq's turn," and a day later, Wolfowitz said that 9/11 created an opportunity to attack Iraq.

The claim that Iraq and Saddam Hussein were involved with 9/11 was based on an alleged meeting that took place between one of the hijackers, Muhammad Atta, and the head of Iraqi intelligence in Prague, in the Czech Republic, in April 2001. Bush and other officials repeated the "story" of that meeting as fact, although there was no evidence that such a meeting had occurred. Vice President Cheney, for example, said that the meeting was "pretty well confirmed." However, then-CIA director George Tenet subsequently told Congress that the United States had no such information. As it became clear that no such meeting had occurred, Bush stopped repeating it in his speeches, but continued to always talk about 9/11 in the same breath as Iraq. This intentional and misleading conflation of 9/11 and Iraq left the American public and Congress with a lie as one of the two bases for the war. Just a few months before the war in the Fall of 2002, 69 percent of the American public believed that Saddam Hussein was responsible for 9/11.

In addition to creating the false impression that Saddam Hussein and 9/11 were connected, the administration, in a two year period, engaged in an all-out effort to prove that Iraq was an imminent threat because it had weapons of mass destruction. President Bush and the administration did so intentionally in order to claim that the war was legal and to obtain the consent of Congress and the American people. In order to do so, however, the administration had to have intelligence demonstrating that Iraq did have such WMDs. As part of the conspiracy to do so, Secretary of Defense Rumsfeld at the Pentagon, in October of 2001, created a special unit called the Counter Terrorism Evaluation Group. That group was set up under Rumsfeld's control so that it could pick and choose intelligence as a means of justifying the claim regarding weapons of mass destruction. It was set up as a means of "finding" intelligence to justify war. The National Intelligence Estimate, prepared by the CIA, stated that Iraq had no nuclear weapons, and was not trying to obtain them. In addition, throughout 2001, administration officials claimed falsely that Iraq was involved with chemical weapons and that it was violating the biological weapons pact.

The year 2002 began with Bush's listing of Iraq, in his State of the Union address, as one of the countries in the "Axis of Evil." A few months into 2002, Cheney and his chief of staff, I. Lewis "Scooter" Libby, made a number of trips to the CIA to discuss intelligence regarding Iraq. Presumably the purpose of those trips was to convince the CIA into bending that intelligence to justify the war. Cheney continued to contend falsely that Iraq had biological weapons in mid-2002. At the same time that the president was planning a war against Iraq, the White House was stating publicly that the U.S. was reluctant to use military force and that it was a last resort. "But the president continues to seek a peaceful resolution. War is a last resort," noted Scott McClellan, in a November 12, 2002 White House press briefing.

One document that has been produced and that demonstrates the dishonesty that was used to justify the Iraq war is the so-called "Downing Street Memo." Dated July 23, 2002, it is a British document summarizing a meeting that Prime Minister Tony Blair had with his cabinet and British intelligence officials. The memo conclusively demonstrates that the Bush administration was misreading and exaggerating intelligence in its efforts to prove that Iraq was involved in terrorism and weapons of mass destruction: "Military action was now seen as inevitable. Bush wanted to remove Saddam, through military action, justified by the conjunction of terrorism and WMD. But the intelligence and facts were being fixed around the policy." The clear conclusion is that the Bush administration was fabricating intelligence to justify a war. As the memo says, "It seemed clear that Bush had made up his mind to take military action." This despite the fact that, as the British Foreign Secretary says in the memo, "the case was thin." As there was no factual basis for the weapons of mass destruction claim, nor for Iraq's involvement in 9/11, there was no legal basis for attacking Iraq. As the British attorney general concluded, "the desire for regime change was not a legal base for military action."

The lies and deceptions of the administration continued throughout 2002. In August 2002, the White House Iraq Group was set up to bolster public support for the war. In that same month, Vice President Cheney gave two speeches in which he "predicted that Iraqi President Saddam Hussein will obtain a nuclear weapon fairly soon." Military experts disputed this estimate, and Cheney provided no basis for it. On September 7, 2002, President Bush said that an International Atomic Energy Agency (IAEA) report indicated that Saddam Hussein was "six months away from developing a [nuclear] weapon." There was no such report.

On September 8, 2002, *The New York Times*, in a report by staffers Michael Gordon and Judith Miller, reported that, according to anonymous "Bush administration officials," "Iraq has stepped up its quest for nuclear weapons and has embarked on a world-wide hunt to make an atomic bomb. Iraq has sought to buy thousands of specially designed aluminum tubes, which American officials believe were intended as components of centrifuges to enrich uranium." (It was subsequently "revealed" by the administration that the tubes were bought from Niger.) On that same date, five top U.S. officials—the vice president, Dick Cheney; two cabinet officers, Donald Rumsfeld and Colin Powell; Condoleezza Rice, the national security adviser; and the chairman of the joint chiefs of staff, Richard Meyers—went on national television programs to talk about Iraq's quest for nuclear weapons. The charges regarding the tubes and the hunt for uranium should not have been given any credibility and were false. In his September 12, 2002, speech to the United Nations, President Bush claimed Saddam would be able to build nuclear weapons within one year. This too was false. Subsequently, an official at the IAEA said the documents detailing the aluminum tube charges "are so bad that I cannot imagine that they came from a serious intelligence agency. It depresses me, given the low quality of the documents, that it was not stopped." On October 3, the CIA informed the White House, "Do not reference Niger

Uranium claim." Despite this, on October 7, Bush claimed in Cincinnati, Ohio, that Iraq was reconstituting its nuclear weapons program (the claim was made in a speech in which he also said that Iraq had trained al Qaeda in the uses of bombs and poison).

All of this administration activity was carried out in the effort to obtain a Congressional resolution authorizing the use of force against Iraq. Such a resolution was obtained on October 10, 2002. The resolution authorized Bush to use force against Iraq, upon his certification that Iraq remained a continuing threat that could not be dealt with diplomatically and by peaceful means. In order to make such a formal determination, President Bush continued to deceive Congress and the American people with regard to Iraq obtaining weapons of mass destruction, as well as its relationship with terrorism.

On January 28, 2003, Bush gave his State of the Union speech, much of which consisted of his justification for wanting to go to war with Iraq. He repeated the story that Iraq was attempting to obtain uranium tubes from Niger as evidence that Iraq was continuing in its effort to build nuclear weapons. He stated this as fact although on January 27, 2003, the IAEA had indicated that the tube story was false.

There is now further evidence that at the time President Bush was claiming Iraq had WMDs, he knew full well that there was no legal basis to attack Iraq: In February 2006, a second "Downing Street Memo" was leaked to the press. The memo, which has yet to be acknowledged by the government of the U.K., details a conversation between President Bush and Prime Minister Tony Blair that took place three days after President Bush's January 28, 2003 State of the Union Speech. The memo makes clear the president's realization that he needed to create a pretext for war. According to the memo, Bush suggested to Blair, "The U.S. was thinking of flying U2 reconnaissance aircraft with fighter cover over Iraq, painted in UN colors. If Saddam fired on them, he would be in breach." Bush also suggests, "It was also possible that a defector could be brought out who would give a public presentation about Saddam's WMD, and there was also a small possibility that Saddam would be assassinated." The president also suggested that should the diplomatic effort fail in the U.N., despite the fact that the U.S. would "twist arms" and "even threaten," that "if ultimately we failed, military action would follow anyway." Thus, in order to achieve his means, the president conspired to orchestrate an international incident, a false presentation to the American people, an assassination, and a war no matter what.

Shortly thereafter, and despite the administration's recognition that it had no legal support to declare war, Secretary of State Colin Powell went before the UN on February 5, 2003, and made what many thought was a powerful case justifying such a war. However, every key contention in his speech was without support. On March 8, ten days prior to the official start of the war, President Bush in a radio address to the American people falsely claimed that he was trying to avoid war: "We are doing everything we can to avoid war in Iraq. But if Saddam Hussein does not disarm peacefully, he will be disarmed by force."

On March 17, three days before the war began, President Bush again lied to the American people. "Intelligence gathered by this and other governments leaves no doubt that the Iraq regime continues to possess and conceal some of the most lethal weapons ever devised. And it [Iraq] has aided, trained, and harbored terrorists, including operatives of al Qaeda." On March 18, 2003, President Bush sent a letter to Congress containing his "determination" that Saddam Hussein remained a "continuing threat," and that diplomacy could not work to disarm him. In addition, he said the use of force was necessary to deal with those responsible for "the terrorist attacks that occurred on September 11, 2001." As we have seen, there was no evidence to support either of these propositions. Congress and the American people were once again lied to, but this time in an official determination by the president that triggered the start of the war.

The Iraq war officially began on March 20, 2003. The war continues today. It has cost the United States well over 2,200 lives so far and eight times that in wounded; Iraqi deaths are put at 30,000 by the lowest estimate (a number which was cited by President Bush in a public talk on December 12, 2005). Based on Congressional appropriations as of this date, the cost of the war so far is approximately $240 billion. Even after the war began, and was supposedly over, President Bush lied to the American people about the reasons for war. For example, in a July 14, 2003, press conference at the White House, the president declared, "The larger point is, and the fundamental question is, did Saddam Hussein have a weapons program? And the answer is, absolutely. And we gave him a chance to allow the inspectors in, and he would not let them in. And, therefore, after a reasonable request, we decided to remove him from power, along with other nations, so as to make sure he was not a threat to the United States and our friends and allies in the region...."

Speaking about impeachment, one of the framers of the Constitution, James Iredell, stated, "The President must certainly be punishable for giving false information to the Senate." And that is precisely what President Bush has done, and more. He has lied to the American people and the Congress as to the basis of the war with Iraq. He has involved the United States and its people in a devastating war that has killed thousands and cost billions. By doing so he has subverted the will of Congress, which alone has the right to declare war, and coerced them into doing so by falsities. He has undermined democracy by painting a false picture of the reasons for war to the American people. He has broken the law, both by committing a fraud on the American people, and by violating the fundamental legal precept prohibiting aggressive wars. He has attempted to end the system upon which our country was founded: that the president is a creature of the Constitution and law and has limited powers that are checked and balanced by the other branches. By issuing false statements and lying to Congress and the American people, he has induced Congress and the American people to enter into a war to which the people may not have consented had the true facts been known to them. By doing so, he has subverted the powers of the Congress that are meant to check presidential power. He has undermined our republican form of government. He has violated the public trust and overstepped the bounds of his office. For these reasons, George W. Bush must be impeached.

ARTICLE III

George W. Bush, in his conduct of the Office of the President of the United States, has abused his power by violating the constitutional and international rights of citizens and non-citizens by arbitrarily detaining them indefinitely inside and outside of the United States, without due process, without charges, and with limited—if any—access to counsel or courts.

George W. Bush has abused his power and failed to faithfully execute the laws of the United States by allowing his administration to condone torture, failing to investigate and prosecute high-level officials responsible for torture, and officially refusing to accept the binding nature of a statutory ban on cruel, inhuman, or degrading treatment or punishment.

George W. Bush has offended our system of government by attempting to expand his power at the expense of the other two branches of government. Wherefore George W. Bush, by such conduct, warrants impeachment and trial, and removal from office.

George W. Bush has authorized indefinite detentions without due process or judicial review until the end of the "war on terror"—a war he acknowledges is without a logical end point. The president has clearly signaled to executive branch officials under his command that there are little to no constitutional or other legal constraints in his "war on terror," especially with regard to the rights of suspects. This sanctioning of lawlessness has resulted in the torture, arbitrary detention, and extraordinary rendition of countless human beings.

George W. Bush has abused his presidential power by permitting the executive branch's use of torture and arbitrary detentions to be shrouded with secrecy and deceit, and has failed to prevent or stop torture and hold those who are truly responsible accountable. In so doing, Bush has betrayed the people of the United States and our Constitution.

SPECIFICATION FIRST. The Bush administration has essentially claimed the right to detain anyone, anywhere, in the "war on terror." Within days of September 11, 2001, hundreds of Muslim non-citizens of Arab or South Asian descent in the U.S. were rounded up by the executive branch and detained through the arbitrary enforcement of minor immigration laws. Many of them were then labeled of "special interest" to the 9/11 criminal investigation, detained until cleared of any connection to terrorism (some were detained up to nine months—long after the expiration of any legitimate immigration purpose), and then deported. They were denied the due process rights they would have been entitled to had they been accused of crimes. Many were held in extremely restrictive confinement and subjected to systematic verbal and physical abuse, including beatings, all of which were documented by the Justice Department's Office of the Inspector General. The Department of Justice refused to provide the identities or locations of post-9/11 detainees in 2001 in response to a specific request by six Senators and members of Congress.

In addition to arbitrarily detaining people in the U.S. on minor immigration violations, the executive used a federal law that permits the arrest and brief detention of "material witnesses" who have important information about a crime if they might otherwise flee to avoid testifying. After 9/11, the Department of Justice detained 70 "material witnesses," 69 of whom were Muslim. Almost half of the witnesses were never brought before a grand jury or court to testify, and only a few were ever charged with crimes related to terrorism.

By executive fiat, George W. Bush has indefinitely detained U.S. citizens in the U.S. without criminal charges, and without access to counsel or the courts, thereby stripping them of their constitutional and human rights. The president designated U.S. citizen Jose Padilla an "enemy combatant" and directed that he be detained in military custody in June 2002. Padilla was arrested in Chicago and was never alleged to be a member of al Qaeda or to have fought for the Taliban. He was said to be attempting to explode a radioactive or "dirty" bomb in the United States.

Nevertheless, the Bush administration held him incommunicado in a U.S. Navy brig in South Carolina for more than three years and denied him access to a lawyer or a court for nearly all of that time. After a court finally ordered the Bush administration to allow Padilla to meet with his lawyers, and the appeals court ruled his detention unconstitutional, the case went up to the Supreme Court, where it was sent back down to another court.

When the time came for the government to show why the president had the power to detain U.S. citizens this way, Padilla was transferred into civilian custody and charged with conspiracy to murder, maim, and kidnap people overseas. The Supreme Court was preparing to hear the case, and the transfer to criminal court appeared to be another effort to avoid judicial review of the president's power to detain U.S. citizens in this way.

Yaser Esam Hamdi, a 23-year-old U.S. citizen born in Louisiana, was captured in Afghanistan and taken to the U.S. Naval base at Guantánamo Bay. Although he was soon brought to the U.S., he continued to be deprived of the right to hear the charges against him, or to be brought before a court. The Bush administration kept him in solitary confinement and without charge on a floating naval brig in Goose Creek, South Carolina. In his case challenging his detention, *Hamdi v. Rumsfeld*, the Supreme Court confirmed that a citizen detainee classified as an "enemy combatant" must receive notice of the factual basis for this determination and be given the opportunity to refute such basis before a neutral decision maker. Justice Sandra Day O'Connor wrote that a "state of war is not a blank check for the president when it comes to the rights of the Nation's citizens." Rather than justify Hamdi's lengthy detention without charge before a neutral decision maker, however, the U.S. government released him, still without charge, subject to a number of conditions, one of which was that he renounce his U.S. citizenship. By the time of his release, the American-born U.S. citizen had been detained by his own government, with no knowledge of the evidence against him, for nearly three years. The argument that the president has the power to enact such detentions against U.S. citizens is unsubstantiated. The Constitution clearly states that a citizen is entitled to "due process."

The scope of the Bush administration's detentions outside the U.S. has been sweeping. According to the *Guardian* newspaper, reports estimate that there are up to 17,000 detainees under U.S. control in Iraq.

In Afghanistan, more than 2,000 people have been detained at the Bagram airbase alone, and more than 10,000 have been captured and released. According to the U.S., as of May 2005, there were more than 500 individuals still in U.S. custody in Afghanistan. Most of those detained in Afghanistan are kept at U.S. military bases for indefinite periods, with no opportunity to challenge their detention and little or no contact with relatives or lawyers. Others have been sent on to Guantánamo Bay, Cuba. The U.S. government claims that 505 detainees still remain at Guantánamo, and that 247 detainees have been released. The more than 750 detainees who ended up at Guantánamo were not just taken from the battlefield in Afghanistan, however, but from countries as far away as Gambia, Zambia, and Bosnia. Even their captors acknowledge that mistakes were made; in widely quoted remarks, Brigadier Martin Lucenti, acting commander of the Guantánamo task force, admitted that "of the 550 [detainees] that we have, I would say most of them, the majority of them, will either be released or transferred to their own countries.... Most of these guys weren't fighting, they were running."

Holding individuals indefinitely without charge and without a determination of their legal status violates the most basic principles of due process according to our domestic law, as well as the equally binding international laws of the Geneva Conventions of 1949. On February 7, 2002, the president issued a memorandum declaring that Taliban and al Qaeda prisoners would not be granted Prisoner of War status under the Geneva Conventions. The president designated the prisoners at Guantánamo "enemy combatants," who could be tried by military commissions operating outside military law and subject to the death penalty. The U.S. government has issued criminal charges against only nine men and, four years after the camp opened, not one trial has begun.

In situations of armed conflict, both international human rights law and humanitarian law apply. As an ICRC commentary on the Fourth Geneva Convention notes, a person captured in the zone of military hostilities "must have some status under international law; he is either a prisoner of war and, as such, covered by the Third Convention, [or] a civilian covered by the Fourth Convention.... There is no intermediate status; nobody in enemy hands can be outside the law." Thus, the Guantánamo detainees are protected by international human rights protections and humanitarian law.

In March 2002, a habeas corpus petition was brought on behalf of four detainees at Guantánamo, *Rasul v. Bush,* which sought to challenge their unlawful detentions. The president argued that U.S. courts did not have jurisdiction over the detainees' habeas petitions because they were being held not in the U.S., but in Guantánamo Bay, Cuba, beyond the reach of law. That issue went to the U.S. Supreme Court, which confirmed in June 2004 that Guantánamo detainees can challenge their detentions in U.S. courts.

Despite the Supreme Court's *Rasul* decision that courts have jurisdiction over the Guantánamo detainees' petitions, the executive has argued in federal court that the detainees have no rights, domestic or international, to be enforced. Just as these issues were about to be decided by the D.C. Court of Appeals, and less than two months after the Supreme Court's decision to determine the enforceability of the Geneva Conventions and the legality of the military commissions, the government attempted to legislatively take away the power of the courts to decide these issues.

On December 30, 2005, the president signed into law the "Detainee Treatment Act of 2005" (DTA), which would strip the courts of the power to hear the Guantánamo detainees' habeas challenges and provide the executive the ability to indefinitely detain people at Guantánamo without any justification. Under the Administration's interpretation, detainees could only access a court for a very narrow set of claims after their initial designation as an "enemy combatant" by a Combatant Status Review Tribunal (CSRT) or after conviction by a military commission, neither of which the administration would be required to conduct. Despite a statutory presumption against retroactivity, the administration stated when he signed the law that the executive branch would construe the law to preclude the federal courts from exercising jurisdiction over any future or existing action. The administration is now seeking to dismiss pending petitions on behalf of the detainees. The habeas stripping provision of the DTA seeks to eliminate the checks and balances of the judicial branch, and is therefore unconstitutional.

SPECIFICATION SECOND. There has long been no doubt that torture is unlawful under any circumstances. Torture violates the Constitution, including the Eighth Amendment prohibition on inflicting cruel and unusual punishments and the Fifth Amendment right to due process, which prohibits conduct that "shocks the conscience." Torture also violates federal statutory law. Torture is a federal crime, as is aiding and abetting, conspiring to, or attempting to torture, even if done outside the U.S., so long as the offender is in the U.S. or is a U.S. national. (This criminal statute defines torture as "an act committed by a person acting under the color of law specifically intended to inflict severe physical or mental pain or suffering...upon another person within his custody or physical control.") The Torture Victim Protection Act of 1991 (TVPA) provides for damages against anyone who subjects another (citizen or non-citizen) to torture or extrajudicial killing under the authority or color of law of a foreign country. The Alien Tort Statute (ATS) permits non-citizens to bring claims for violations of customary international law norms that include torture and extrajudicial killing.

Torture is defined by the TVPA as any act against someone in the "offender's custody or physical control, by which severe pain or suffering... whether physical or mental, is intentionally inflicted on that individual for such purposes as obtaining from that individual or a third person information or a confession, punishing,...intimidating or coercing that individual or a third person, or for any reason based on discrimination of any kind."

According to reports, the detainees at Guantánamo have not only been subject to indefinite detention for more than four years, but most have been isolated in constantly lit cells about 5 x 10 feet, are let out from 10-20 minutes per week to exercise, have virtually no contact with their family or the outside world, and are often held in solitary confinement, some for more than a year. Detainees have been punched and kneed, shackled and repeatedly picked up and dropped, resulting in serious injuries. Detainees have been strangled, and have had lit cigarettes put in their ears. In addition to being beaten, they have been deprived of sleep, exposed to temperature extremes, and subject to sexual and religious humiliation. They have been threatened with rape and other torture, execution, and harm to their families. According to Physicians for Human Rights, the detainees have suffered debilitating psychological effects that include depression, anger, suicidal thoughts and behavior, memory loss, delusions, hallucinations, and sometimes paranoia.

To protest their detentions and mistreatment, detainees have undertaken hunger strikes, to which the Bush Administration has responded by involuntarily and violently force-feeding the detainees through nasal tubes. A tube the size of a finger is forcibly shoved up a detainee's nose, down his throat and into his stomach. Guards have removed tubes by stepping on one end of the tube and pulling the detainee's head back by his hair. The tubes are inserted and removed twice daily, causing profuse bleeding from the nose, severe throat legions, and vomiting of blood. Dirty equipment is used in an unsterile environment, and sometimes tubes are removed from one detainee and reinserted into another without cleaning the blood and stomach bile that remains after removal.

The Bush administration has attempted to justify its detention of Guantánamo prisoners in the CSRTs and the habeas proceedings with information it obtains though torture. Information obtained through torture is not only recognized as not credible, but using information obtained through torture in legal proceedings is prohibited by the U.S. Constitution and the Convention Against Torture and Other Cruel Inhuman or Degrading Treatment or Punishment (CAT), an international treaty ratified by the U.S. The Inter-American Commission on Human Rights has asked the U.S. not to permit such statements to be used in proceedings, in accordance with international law. To date, the U.S. has disregarded the Commission's recommendations as well as American law.

The president has repeatedly disregarded the condemnation of abuses at Guantánamo by international bodies. Since 2002 the International Committee for the Red Cross (ICRC) has visited Guantánamo to monitor whether the treatment of prisoners accords with international law. After its visit in the summer of 2004, it found evidence of abuse "tantamount to torture," and met with President Bush to discuss concerns about prisoners' detentions. The UN Special Rapporteur on Torture, the expert appointed by the United Nations Commission on Human Rights to examine questions related to torture, has corroborated that allegations of cruelty are "well-substantiated." A group of five UN Special Rapporteurs were forced to cancel an inspection visit to Guantánamo scheduled for December 2005, after the U.S. refused to agree to allow private contact with the prisoners. President Bush has denied allegations of abuse.

Several groups, including the ICRC, the Army, and the Department of Defense, investigated and documented the physical, sexual, and psychological abuse of prisoners at Abu Ghraib Prison. Sworn statements from detainees and innumerable news reports provided further documentation. Prisoners were regularly beaten; one was beaten with a chair until it broke, and was kicked and choked until he lost consciousness. Another detainee was beaten with a broom, had a liquid chemical poured all over him, and was sodomized with a police stick while two female MPs threw a ball at his genitals and took photographs. One detainee witnessed the rape of a teenage prisoner while a female soldier took photographs.

Psychological abuse, intimidation, and degradation were pervasive at Abu Ghraib, especially forced nakedness to interrogate, punish, and dehumanize detainees. Detainees were left naked, hooded, and chained to the doors of their cells. Boys were stripped and cuffed together facing each other. Masturbation was also frequently forced on groups and individuals. One Army report details detainees being placed in a pile and told to masturbate, then being "ridden like animals." Prisoners were further humiliated by having women see their genitals, being urinated on, and having their food thrown in the toilet. Prisoners were placed in solitary confinement with poor air quality and extreme temperatures and were also intimidated and threatened. One detainee told of having electrical wires placed on his fingers, toes, and penis and being threatened with electrocution. The aforementioned Army report notes dogs were placed in the cell of juvenile prisoners and permitted to "go nuts."

In Afghanistan, detainees were also tortured and subject to cruel, inhuman, or degrading treatment or punishment (CIDTP). Released detainees describe being continuously shackled, held naked, intentionally kept awake for extended periods of time, and being forced to kneel or stand in painful positions for extended periods. Some allege that they were kicked or beaten, others that they were doused with freezing water in the winter. In a *Wall Street Journal* report, military interrogators admit: "Interrogators can also play on their prisoners' phobias, such as fear of rats or dogs, or disguise themselves as interrogators from a country known to use torture or threaten to send the prisoners to such a place. Prisoners can be stripped, forcibly shaved and deprived of religious items and toiletries."

At least seven Afghan detainees have been killed in U.S. custody, including two men killed in December 2002 by "blunt force injuries," according to their death certificates. Despite the death certificates, the Army said that both men died of heart failure. Its investigation into the deaths implicated 28 men; charges have been proffered against only two. The Department of Defense has yet to explain adequately the circumstances of any of the seven deaths, and, unlike Iraq, almost no information is publicly available regarding any potential U.S. investigations or prosecutions of military personnel.

Torture is proscribed universally and is not officially sanctioned by any nation; any use of torture violates customary international law, which is binding on all nations, regardless of their assent. Torture is prohibited by the Universal Declaration of Human Rights, the paramount international human rights statement adopted unanimously by the United Nations General Assembly in 1948. Torture and other cruel, inhuman or degrading treatment or punishment is also prohibited by international treaties ratified by the United States, including CTA and The International Covenant on Civil and Political Rights (ICCPR). These treaties make clear that an individual's right to be protected from torture cannot be suspended under any circumstances, even in times of national emergency.

Cruel inhuman or degrading treatment or punishment is generally considered to include acts which inflict mental or physical suffering, anguish, humiliation, fear, and debasement that fall short of torture or do not share its purpose. The Inter-American Declaration on the Rights and Duties of Man, to which the U.S. is bound by its membership in the Organization of American States, also prohibits the use of cruel or inhumane treatment against individuals. International Humanitarian Law, which places restrictions on the conduct of warfare, also forbids torture. The Third and Fourth Geneva Conventions specifically ban the use of torture against prisoners of war and protected persons, respectively, during times of armed conflict.

The president's February 7, 2002 memorandum stated that the U.S. Armed Forces must treat prisoners humanely only "to the extent appropriate and consistent with military necessity." That directive to treat prisoners humanely, notwithstanding its qualification, expressly applied to the Armed

Forces, not the CIA and other nonmilitary personnel, which then-counsel to the president, Alberto Gonzales, confirmed to the Senate Judiciary Committee. He also informed the committee that the president believed the prohibition on CIDTP does not apply to non-citizens held outside the U.S. Gonzales, who had also produced a January 25, 2002 memorandum to the president stating that the war on terrorism made some provisions of the Geneva Conventions "quaint," and rendered "obsolete" their "strict limitations on questioning of enemy prisoners," was nominated by the president and subsequently confirmed to be attorney general.

Another executive branch memorandum argued that the prohibition on torture didn't apply to the "war on terror," and that in case it did, the definition of torture was narrowed as to be almost meaningless; the August 1, 2002 Office of Legal Counsel memorandum from Jay S. Bybee to Alberto R. Gonzales was just one of many memoranda issued by the executive branch to excise its treatment of detainees from the law. Among other legally unsound advice, this memorandum concluded that in order to constitute torture, pain must be akin to that accompanying "serious physical injury, such as organ failure, impairment of bodily function, or even death." The memorandum also concluded that even if an act constituted torture under that definition, applying the criminal statutory ban on torture may be unconstitutional if applied to "interrogations undertaken pursuant to the President's Commander-in-Chief powers," and that "necessity or self-defense could provide justifications that would eliminate any criminal liability." In other words, the president's lawyers advised that the ban on torture is limited to "extreme forms" of harm, and that there were arguments to get around liability regardless. The Pentagon's March 6, 2003 "Working Group Report on Detainee Interrogations in the Global War on Terrorism: Assessment of Legal, Historical, Policy, and Operational Considerations" also found that the criminal prohibition against torture did not apply to detentions and interrogations conducted pursuant to the president's commander-in-chief authority.

The August 2002 Bybee memorandum was "superseded" in its entirety by a December 30, 2004 memorandum which disagreed with each of these conclusions and various other assertions. (A subsequent memorandum disagreed with the August 2002 statements that mental harm would have to last for at least "months or even years" to be considered prolonged, and that infliction of severe pain or suffering is not torture if it was not the "precise objective" of the action, even if it was certain or reasonably likely to result.) Despite these disagreements, the December memorandum stated that, "we have reviewed this Office's prior opinions addressing issues involving treatment of detainees and do not believe that any of their conclusions would be different under the standards set forth in this memorandum." In other words, the techniques authorized pursuant to the looser, unlawful standard should still be considered lawful under the revised standard. Congress passed the DTA in December 2005 explicitly stating that "No individual in the custody or under the physical control of the United States Government...shall be subject to cruel, inhuman, or degrading treatment or punishment." Despite the administration's efforts to prevent passage of the provision, incorporate a presidential waiver, or at least exempt CIA employees from the legislation, the CIDTP prohibition passed, and contained no exceptions.

Perhaps because the CIDTP prohibition was attached to the 2006 National Defense Authorization Bill (authorizing the year's funding for military and defense activities), the president did not have much choice but to sign the bill into law, but he consequently issued a "signing statement" expressing his opinion that he can essentially disregard the prohibition on CIDTP to prevent "terrorist attacks." "The Executive branch shall construe the act...in a manner consistent with...protecting the American people from further terrorist attacks." To bolster that pronouncement, the president emphasized that a victim of the violation of the new law couldn't sue under it anyway since it did not "create a private right of action." It was an unprecedented flaunting of an explicit and universal prohibition by Congress. (The president's use of "signing statements" has been sweeping—in his first term alone, he implemented more than double the prior number of such statements throughout the history of the presidency—435 statements as compared to 322 total statements by all previous presidents. In these statements and in his executive orders, the president used the term "unitary executive" 95 times.)

Despite overwhelming evidence of torture, and the fact that public high-level legal memoranda have essentially condoned torture, the Bush administration has failed to investigate, much less prosecute higher-level officials, and has attempted to conceal their responsibility and limited investigations to lower-level officials. The president has instead promoted high-level officials responsible for the torture and ill-treatment of detainees.

Regardless of whether the president himself authorized the use of torture, he has responsibility for those under his command. Under the legal principle of command responsibility, superior officers are liable for the criminal actions of their subordinates when they knew or should have known that crimes were being committed, but failed to take adequate and appropriate measures to prevent them, failed to punish them, or ratified them. The president rejected application of the Geneva Conventions, sanctioned memoranda essentially condoning torture, promoted and failed to investigate and prosecute high-level officials responsible for torture, and contests a congressional admonishment to ban all cruel, inhuman, or degrading treatment or punishment.

SPECIFICATION THIRD. On September 17, 2001, the president issued a classified directive, or "presidential finding," authorizing the CIA to capture and detain (or kill) members of al Qaeda anywhere in the world. It is also reported that the president gave the CIA broad authority to act without case-by-case approval to transfer detainees to the custody of foreign nations. The CIA has no law enforcement powers, so cannot legally arrest or detain anyone; but since 9/11, the CIA has covertly abducted people and delivered them to other countries to be detained and interrogated through torture, a practice sometimes called "Extraordinary Renditions."

The practice of "rendition" had been authorized to bring someone from another country (with its permission) to stand trial for a crime—to bring someone with an outstanding arrest warrant or conviction to justice, albeit outside of an extradition treaty. Under the Bush administration, rendition has mutated into a practice whereby the CIA covertly abducts suspects, flies them on private jets to other countries to be secretly held captive without any due process, and interrogated through torture. U.S. officials have picked up people from countries that include Sweden, Germany, Italy, and Macedonia, and taken them to other countries known to torture suspects, like Egypt, Jordan, Syria, Saudi Arabia, Afghanistan, and Pakistan, all of which have been identified by the U.S. State Department as routinely using torture on prisoners. Because the practice is covert, it is not publicly known how many people the executive branch has sent to other countries to be detained and tortured, although estimates range from 150 to the thousands.

Attorney General Alberto Gonzales has admitted publicly that once a transfer occurs "we can't fully control what that country might do. We obviously expect a country to which we have rendered a detainee to comply with their representations to us. If you're asking me 'Does a country always comply?' I don't have an answer to that." CIA Director Porter Goss also admitted in congressional testimony the inability to enforce diplomatic assurances: "We have a responsibility of trying to ensure that they are properly treated, and we try and do the best we can to guarantee that. But of course once they're out of our control, there's only so much we can do."

A German citizen of Lebanese descent, Khaled El-Masri, was abducted on December 31, 2003, while on a trip in Macedonia. U.S. agents beat and drugged him, and flew him to a secret prison in Afghanistan, where he was kept in a U.S. prison facility, beaten and kicked and interrogated repeatedly. He was kept in Afghanistan for five months, before being flown to Albania and abandoned at night on a hilltop.

On June 17, 2003, an Egyptian citizen, Hassam Osama Mustafa Nasr, known as Abu Omar, was abducted in Milan, Italy. He was a political refugee who was under surveillance by the Milan government, but was seized by the CIA without the consent, or even the prior knowledge, of the Italian authorities. Abu Omar was flown via Germany to Egypt, where he was tortured before being released and re-arrested. An Italian judicial investigation established beyond all reasonable doubt that the operation was carried out by the CIA, and 22 warrants for the arrest of the CIA agents who abducted Abu Omar have been issued in Milan.

Maher Arar, a Canadian citizen born in Syria, was picked up in September 2002 while transiting through New York's JFK airport on his way home to Canada. Immigration and FBI officials detained and interrogated him for nearly two weeks and interfered with his rights to access counsel, the Canadian consulate, and the courts. Executive branch officials asked him if he would volunteer to go to Syria, where he hadn't been in 15 years, and Maher refused. It is well documented that Syria has an extremely poor human rights record and the Department of State has often reported that Syria tortures people as an interrogation tool. According to Vincent Cannistraro, a former CIA counterterrorism official, "'You would have to be deaf, dumb and blind to believe that the Syrians were not going to use torture, even if they were making claims to the contrary.'"

Maher was put on a private jet plane to Jordan, where he was beaten for eight hours, and then delivered to Syria, where he was beaten and interrogated for 18 hours a day for weeks. He was whipped on his back and hands with a 2-inch thick electric cable and asked questions similar to those he had been asked in the United States. For over ten months Maher was held in an underground grave like cell—3 x 6 x 7 feet—it was damp and cold, and the only light came in through a hole in the ceiling. After a year in Syria, Maher was released without any charges and is now back home in Canada with his family. Upon his release, the Syrian government announced he had no links to al Qaeda, and the Canadian government has also said they've found no links to al Qaeda. The Canadian government launched a Commission of Inquiry into the Actions of Canadian Officials in Relation to Maher Arar, to investigate the role of Canadian officials, but the Bush administration has refused to cooperate with the inquiry.

In January 2004, Maher brought suit in U.S. court against the U.S. officials responsible for sending him to Syria to be tortured, including former Attorney General Ashcroft, former Deputy Attorney General Larry Thompson, FBI Director Robert Mueller, and several immigration officials. The government officials moved to dismiss the case. The executive branch has taken the unusual measure of asking the U.S. court to dismiss the bulk of Maher's case, claiming litigation would disclose "state secrets," harming national security and foreign relations. This is another of the extraordinary means the Bush administration has gone to in an attempt to increase its power to act outside of the law. If accepted, the "state secrets" assertion could also prevent adjudication of the use of secret prisons, torture, or even assassinations anywhere around the world. The establishment of detention and interrogation prisons at Guantánamo, and in secret locations outside of the U.S., has already obstructed judicial review, thereby violating the constitutional separation of powers.

The same U.S. laws prohibiting aiding and abetting torture also prohibit sending someone to a country where there is a substantial likelihood they may be tortured. International treaties also prohibit "extraordinary renditions." CAT prohibits sending someone to a country where there is a "substantial likelihood" that an individual "may be in danger" of torture, and has been implemented by a federal statute. The ICCPR prohibits sending individuals to where they may be "at risk" of either torture or cruel, inhuman, or degrading treatment.

In the context of armed conflicts, transferring a POW to a nation where he is likely to be tortured or inhumanely treated violates Article 12 of the Third Geneva Convention, and transferring a civilian who is a protected person under the Fourth Geneva Convention is a grave breach and a criminal act. The ICRC's commentary on the 1949 conventions states that prisoners should not be repatriated where there are serious reasons for fearing that repatriating the individual would be contrary to general principals of established international law for the protection of human beings.

In 2002 and 2003, reportedly justified as within the scope of the president's authorization, the CIA brokered deals with other countries to allow "black sites"—secret detention facilities outside the U.S.—to be set up. Senior U.S. officials requested that *The Washington Post,* when it learned of these sites, not publish the European countries in which the prisons were located. The locations of these facilities are known only to the president and key operatives in the U.S., and the head of state and high-level intelligence personnel in the host countries. Most of the facilities were built and are maintained with congressionally appropriated funds, but the White House has refused to allow the CIA to brief anyone except the House and Senate intelligence committees' chairmen and vice chairmen on the program's generalities.

News stories in *The New York Times* and elsewhere report that the CIA is holding approximately 36 high ranking leaders of al Qaeda in secret sites overseas. The United States has acknowledged the detention of many, but almost certainly not all, and has not only refused them access to the International Committee of the Red Cross, their lawyers and their families, but has consistently refused to say even where they are being held.

There are also "ghost detainees" held at known detention centers, but kept off the prison's roster, and out of sight of the ICRC: In June 2004, Secretary Rumsfeld admitted that, acting on a request by the CIA, he had ordered an Iraqi national to be held in a high security detention center in Iraq and not presented to the International Committee of the Red Cross. An Army report into intelligence activities at Abu Ghraib spoke of eight "ghost" detainees there, kept off the roster at the CIA's request, one of whom died at the site. His body was removed after being wrapped in plastic, and packed in ice.

After the existence of prisons in Eastern Europe became known, the UN Special Rapporteur on Torture expressed concern and said that he would be requesting more information from the government. The E.U. is asking questions of its 25 member states, and the Council of Europe, Europe's leading human rights organization has opened an investigation to find out more about the prisons, the existence of which, it says, violates both international law and the European Convention on Human Rights.

The president took detainees to Guantánamo to avoid public and judicial scrutiny, and when the Supreme Court confirmed that the detainees could challenge their detentions in U.S. courts, the president argued that the detainees have no rights to be enforced, whether domestic or international. Now the president is attempting to preclude judicial review by trying to eliminate all habeas relief for Guantánamo detainees.

Similarly, the administration is trying to preclude review of "extraordinary rendition" by challenging Maher Arar's case, claiming the court must defer to the executive's assertion that the case cannot be litigated because it would harm national security. This is a fundamental abrogation of the executive's obligations in a system that relies on the judiciary to check the executive's power. While touting the value of healthy democratic debate, the government refuses to disclose allegations against those it arbitrarily detains and renders, claiming those secrets would endanger us if they came out. As the government officially condemns torture, it talks about hard choices and averting attacks and otherwise implies that torture may be justifiable. There simply can be no democratic debate with such secrecy, and there can be no justice without judicial review.

The president has refused to apply the Geneva Conventions to detainees, authorized the inhumane treatment of prisoners, registered his contempt for the will of Congress by stating his intent to ignore the prohibition on CIDTP, and failed to stop the use of torture. The dictates of the Constitution are clear that these are all impeachable offenses.

ARTICLE IV

George W. Bush, in his conduct of the Office of the President of the United States, in violation of his constitutional oath to faithfully execute the Office of President of the United States and, to the best of his ability, preserve, protect, and defend the Constitution of the United States, and in violation of his constitutional duty to take care that the laws be faithfully executed, has arrogated excessive power to the executive branch in violation of basic constitutional principles of the separation of powers.

This conduct has included one or more of the following:

He has violated federal law by conducting surveillance of U.S. citizens on U.S. soil without a judicial warrant, as is required by the Foreign Intelligence Surveillance Act (FISA), which was specifically enacted to check executive power.

He has engaged in mass detentions both in and outside of the United States without permitting any judicial review of such detentions.

He has formally declared his intent to violate the laws enacted by Congress by appending a "signing statement" to legislation that asserts his right to carve out exceptions to legislation as he sees fit, thereby arrogating to himself legislative powers reserved solely to Congress.

In all of this, George W. Bush has acted in a manner contrary to his trust as president and subversive of constitutional government, to the great prejudice of the cause of law and justice and to the manifest injury of the people of the United States. Wherefore George W. Bush, by such conduct, warrants impeachment and trial, and removal from office.

The president does not have absolute power. The power of the president is limited in two fundamental ways.

First, the power of the federal government is divided between the three branches of government—executive, legislative, and judicial. They are referred to as separate and co-equal. One branch may not trod on prerogatives of the other. This is known as "separation of powers." The president's principal duty is to "execute" the laws, not to make them. That is the fundamental purview of the legislature. Nor is the president authorized to provide final interpretations of the laws. That is the fundamental purview of the judiciary.

Second, the power of the president is circumscribed. Individuals have rights that the government may not trammel. The Bill of Rights sets forth fundamental limitations on governmental power, protecting individuals of all persuasions and beliefs, and is the very hallmark of the U.S. system.

These two limits are at the heart of our Constitution. Without them, the republic does not exist.

SPECIFICATION FIRST. As established above, the constitutional principle of separation of powers places limits on presidential power and is a basic feature of our constitutional system. The central reason why the framers included the power to impeach the president in the Constitution was to prevent executive tyranny. Further, the critical phrase in the impeachment clause, "other high Crimes and Misdemeanors," was added by the framers to address cases where a president "attempts to subvert the Constitution." Even more, the impeachment power is understood to encompass the "great offenses" under English common law, one of which was encroachment onto the prerogatives of the other branches of government. Thus, any attempt to undo the separation of powers by the president constitutes a paradigmatic case for impeachment.

The framers created two other constitutional provisions to guard against presidential excess or wrongdoing. The first is the oath, contained in Article II, Section 1 of the Constitution. It defines the basic purpose of the Office of the President. The oath establishes that the president is wholly a creature of the Constitution. The president's role is to "to execute the Office of the President," as defined by the Constitution, and to "preserve, protect, and defend the Constitution of the United States." A failure to "preserve, protect, and defend the Constitution" would violate the oath. Intentionally subverting or undermining the Constitution would constitute something even more serious—a possible perversion of the oath.

The second provision, at Article II, Section 3, known as the Take Care Clause, requires that the president "shall take care that the Laws be faithfully executed." The clause underscores that the president is duty bound to adhere to the law.

In light of these constitutional safeguards, we can examine the actions of George W. Bush.

Concerning the judiciary: According to Justice Department figures, thousands of people throughout the United States were detained during the period after September 11, 2001. Many were held for months, provided with no access to lawyers, and were beaten while in custody. They were not formally charged and were literally "disappeared" in the sense that they were not allowed to communicate with the outside, and their family members did not know where they were held, or whether they were dead or alive. Out of the thousands of detainees, few were ultimately charged with any terrorism-related offense.

Under a U.S. Supreme Court opinion, *County of Riverside v. McLaughin*, 500 U.S. 44, 47 (1991), any person detained by the government must be brought before a magistrate judge within 48 hours so that the appropriateness of their detention may be reviewed. The administration violated the law, failing to bring detainees before a judge for weeks and months. It thus grossly violated basic separation of powers principles by denying the judiciary any opportunity to review thousands of detentions, affecting thousands of detainees, hundreds of judges in hundreds of jurisdictions, and damaging the very notion of a president that must work within a constitutional system.

To the argument that impeachment is not warranted because this is a time of war, and that therefore traditional constitutional limits on the executive no longer apply, there are several significant precedents establishing otherwise. Most notably, just after the Civil War, in which large portions of the United States were physically under rebel control, the Supreme Court in the 1866 case of *Ex Parte Milligan* held that the Constitution applied equally in times of war and in peace:

> The Constitution of the United States is a law for rulers and people, equally in war and in peace, and covers with the shield of its protection all classes of men, at all times, and under all circumstances. No doctrine, involving more pernicious consequences, was ever invented by the wit of man than that any of its provisions can be suspended during any of the great exigencies of government. Such a doctrine leads directly to anarchy or despotism, but the theory of necessity on which it is based is false; for the government, within the Constitution, has all the powers granted to it which are necessary to preserve its existence, as has been happily proved by the result of the greatest effort to throw off its just authority.

The detentions at Guantánamo present a different issue. Detainees there were denied the right to challenge their detention in the courts for years until the administration's position was held unconstitutional by the Supreme Court in *Rasul v. Bush*. Immediately before and just after the ruling, dozens of detainees, who had been alleged to be dangerous terrorists, were simply released. On leaving Guantánamo, many gave credible accounts of being tortured.

These practices of indefinite detention and torture might be defensible with the argument that some illegalities must be tolerated in favor of a achieving a greater good. This argument fails, however, for the end was never achieved: Actionable intelligence was not received, and the mass domestic detentions yielded no relevant charges. And thus the means were deployed for naught, at great damage to the U.S. Even further, the basic safeguards against executive abuse mean little in times of ease. It is only in times of war that they have any function at all, and it is precisely at those times when they must be most observed. Turning to domestic spying and wiretapping, the administration has again broken federal law. According to Senator Arlen Specter, the Republican chair of the Senate Judiciary Committee, the domestic warrantless wiretapping "is a flat violation of the Foreign Intelligence Surveillance Act (FISA)." The next question is of substantiality—whether this illegal act threatens our system of constitutional government. Because of the particular, unusual nature of FISA, the answer is yes.

FISA was specifically enacted to serve as a check on executive power in response to abuses in the 1960s and '70s. It established a special court, from which the executive is required to receive a warrant before engaging in domestic spying. It is important to note that FISA already allows the executive a great deal of latitude: FISA does not flatly prohibit domestic eavesdropping or domestic spying. Rather, it only requires that the executive go before a special, confidential court, one which has historically served as a rubber stamp, granting such warrants in over 99 percent of requests, before or within 72 hours of commencing surveillance.

George W. Bush nonetheless chose to bypass the special FISA court, denying it all judicial review. This circumvention gained the administration no apparent material advantage, as the FISA procedures were liberal to the point of being nonexistent. The only discernible reason is a simple contempt for the principle that executive power can be limited in any way by the judiciary. But to hold this position is to deny the most basic type of separation of powers principles and to subvert our very system of constitutional government. An executive unchecked by the judiciary is simply not a feature of our system. As such, this is an impeachable offense.

While warrantless wiretapping clearly encroaches on the judiciary, it also intrudes on the legislature. Congress spoke in enacting FISA. By violating FISA, the president is violating the expressed will of Congress. The illegal wiretapping also contravenes the Take Care Clause of the Constitution, which requires the president to "take care that the Laws be faithfully executed."

Further evidence of the president's intention to impermissibly arrogate power to the executive at the expense of the legislature can be seen in the "Signing Statement" that he attempted to place on the recent federal anti-torture legislation. That statement read: "The executive branch shall construe [the law] in a manner consistent with the constitutional authority of the President... as Commander in Chief." In essence, the president was asserting that he had the right to carve out his own exceptions to the law, and that he could commit torture when he saw fit. Attempting to justify such a practice, Vice President Dick Cheney told reporters, "I believe in a strong, robust executive authority, and I think that the world we live in demands it.... I would argue that the actions that we've taken are totally appropriate and consistent with the constitutional authority of the president."

Such a scheme would constitute an upending of the basic structure for enacting law that is laid out by the Constitution. The Congress enacts legislation, while the president executes it. That is the schema set out by the first two articles of the Constitution and the very basis of our system of government. The presidential role with regard to legislation is limited to the veto power. The Signing Statement is an attempt by the president to arrogate to himself the power to make laws. The only possible interpretation is that this is a clear and unapologetic attempt to subvert the basic constitutional scheme of the separation of powers.

SPECIFICATION SECOND. Impeachable, or potentially impeachable offenses are usually framed in the public imagination as specific, discrete, nearly tangible acts—authorizing a break-in at a hotel, impermissibly firing a Cabinet official, perjuring oneself in a deposition. Any one such act, if found to rise to the level of "Treason, Bribery, and other high Crimes and Misdemeanors," can be grounds for an impeachment.

But what about a generalized pattern of constitutional subversion? As a Nixon-era report about the history of impeachment from the House Inquiry Staff states:

> "Not all presidential misconduct is sufficient to constitute grounds
> for impeachment. There is a further requirement—substantiality.
> In deciding whether this further requirement has been met,
> *the facts must be considered as a whole in the context of the office,*
> *not in terms of separate or isolated events.* Because impeachment of
> a president is a grave step for the nation, it is to be predicated only
> upon *conduct seriously incompatible with either the constitutional*
> *form and principles of our government* or the proper performance
> of constitutional duties of the presidential office."

In the case of George W. Bush, there has been an inversion of basic constitutional doctrines and principles on a number of fronts. As the judiciary can only deal with cases individually, as they arise, and on the discrete issues they present, it does not have the chance to address, assess, or make sense of the complete constitutional picture.

That picture would have to include the following: The mass detention and disappearances of immigrants. The special registration of immigrants in violation of equal protection guarantees. The failure to execute basic duties and acts of profound neglect in the response to Hurricane Katrina. The launching of an illegal war. The wiretapping of U.S. citizens in contravention of FISA. The abuse and torture of detainees on the mainland, in Guantánamo, and in Iraq. The articulation and defense of a policy in favor of torture, in contravention of an archetypal norm basic to any legal order and civilized society. The imprisonment of humans on the sole and unreviewable word of the president. The abrogation of signed treaties, which the Constitution sets forth as the law of the land. The denial of the right to counsel to detainees, including U.S. citizens on U.S. soil.

Many of these acts have already been ruled unconstitutional. Many of the acts were clearly unconstitutional from the outset. In proposing to legalize torture, for example, the administration was seeking to twist the very nature of the idea of law. Yet due to the nature of the litigation process, the unconstitutionality persists for years as cases wind through the courts. And yet, even where its actions have been reversed by the courts, the administration is unapologetic, and continues to advocate, and use, and expand upon, many of the same practices and ends. The ultimate bulwark against the abuse of executive power, the last line of self-defense for the Constitution, as envisioned by the Founders, is the mechanism of impeachment.

APPENDIX

THE PRESIDENTIAL OATH OF OFFICE

"I do solemnly swear (or affirm) that I will faithfully execute the Office of President of the United States, and will to the best of my Ability, preserve, protect and defend the Constitution of the United States."

—In accordance with the U.S. Constitution
(Article II, Section 2, Clause 3)

WHAT THE CONSTITUTION
SAYS ABOUT IMPEACHMENT

ARTICLE I, SECTION 2.

CLAUSE 5: The House of Representatives shall chuse their Speaker and other Officers; and shall have the sole Power of Impeachment.

ARTICLE I, SECTION 3.

CLAUSE 6: The Senate shall have the sole Power to try all Impeachments. When sitting for that Purpose, they shall be on Oath or Affirmation. When the President of the United States is tried, the Chief Justice shall preside: And no Person shall be convicted without the Concurrence of two thirds of the Members present.

CLAUSE 7: Judgment in Cases of Impeachment shall not extend further than to removal from Office, and disqualification to hold and enjoy any Office of honor, Trust or Profit under the United States: but the Party convicted shall nevertheless be liable and subject to Indictment, Trial, Judgment and Punishment, according to Law.

ARTICLE II, SECTION 2.

CLAUSE 1: ...and [the president] shall have Power to grant Reprieves and Pardons for Offences against the United States, except in Cases of Impeachment.

ARTICLE II, SECTION 4.

The President, Vice President and all civil Officers of the United States, shall be removed from Office on Impeachment for, and Conviction of, Treason, Bribery, or other high Crimes and Misdemeanors.

ARTICLE III, SECTION 2.

CLAUSE 3: The Trial of all Crimes, except in Cases of Impeachment, shall be by Jury, . . .

THE HISTORY OF IMPEACHMENT

"Guilt wherever found ought to be punished," said Edmund Randolph, governor of Virginia and delegate to the Constitutional Convention. His remarks, made on July 20, 1787, were in support of including provisions for impeachment in the U.S. Constitution. "The Executive will have great opportunitys of abusing his power; particularly in time of war when the military force, and in some respects the public money will be in his hands. Should no regular punishment be provided, it will be irregularly inflicted by tumults and insurrections."[1]

Most in attendance at the Convention had a similar passion for including provisions for impeachment in the Constitution. Having broken free from the monarchy, the framers wanted a way to ensure that the people would never again fall prey to the whims of absolute power. If the United States was to be governed by the people, they argued, impeachment must be included in the Constitution as a way to keep those in power true to their word to uphold the people's will.

Rooted in English law and in use as early as the 1300s, the impeachment process was devised by the British Parliament as a way to hold its ground against the king. It proved especially important when it came to those he appointed. If the king's minions abused their power or were derelict in their duties, there could frequently be no way to ensure their removal from office except for impeachment.[2] At the time of the Constitutional Convention, Americans were following the Parliament's trial of Warren Hastings, governor general of India, who was impeached on charges of oppression, bribery, and fraud, so there is no doubt that impeachment was very much in the framers' collective conscience.[3] The framers, in fact, replicated the parliamentary impeachment process: A vote to impeach must be introduced and approved in the lower house, or House of Representatives, and then the impeachment is tried in the upper house, or Senate.

During the Convention, however, there was debate over the need to include impeachment in the Constitution. Some wondered if impeachment was truly necessary since there would be strict terms of office. James Madison, future president and known as the "architect" of the Constitution, argued the importance of impeachment, especially as it applied to the executive branch. "The case of the Executive Magistracy was very distinguishable, from that of the Legislature or of any other public body, holding offices of limited duration," he said. "Besides the restraints of their personal integrity and honor, the difficulty of acting in concert for purposes of corruption was a security to the public. And if one or a few members only should be seduced, the soundness of the remaining members, would maintain the integrity and fidelity of the body. In the case of the Executive Magistracy which was to be administered by a single man, loss of capacity or corruption was more within the compass of probable events, and either of them might be fatal to the Republic."[4]

But what should constitute an impeachable offense? Here the framers looked again to the British Parliament's use of impeachment, especially with regard to phrasing. The language first proposed included only bribery and treason, both of which were clearly defined in the Constitution. But George Mason, delegate from Virginia, argued that these offenses did not go far enough: "Why is the provision restrained to Treason & bribery only?" he said. "Treason as defined in the Constitution will not reach many great and dangerous offences .... Attempts to subvert the Constitution may not be Treason as above defined."⁵ In light of this, he suggested that after treason and bribery, "maladministration" should be added.

James Madison objected to "maladministration," however, arguing "So vague a term will be equivalent to a tenure during pleasure of the Senate."⁶ His fear was that the legislative branch, responsible for the impeachment process, could invoke impeachment for practically anything using the term "maladministration," thereby wielding too much power over the executive branch. In response, Mason proposed that the language should read "treason, bribery, or other High Crimes and Misdemeanors," which was ultimately adopted. The phrase "High Crimes and Misdemeanors" was not, however, language then in use in the criminal courts, and Mason's use of "misdemeanor" should not be confused with the current legal sense of the term. The phrase "High Crimes and Misdemeanors" was generally understood at the time of the Constitution's drafting as it was used in Parliament to cover a myriad of offenses whereby an official has overstepped the particular bounds of public office. Such a crime may or may not be punishable under common law but must always be a grave and immediate offense against the state.⁷

Alexander Hamilton referred to impeachable offenses in *The Federalist Papers* as "those offences which proceed from the misconduct of public men, or, in other words, from the abuse or violation of some public trust. They are of a nature which may with peculiar propriety be denominated *POLITICAL*, as they relate chiefly to injuries done immediately to the society itself."⁸

Only two U.S. presidents have been impeached, Andrew Johnson (1868) and William Jefferson Clinton (1999). Both impeachments occurred during times of heightened tension between political parties.

Eleven articles of impeachment were brought against Johnson, including "inflammatory, and scandalous harangues" against Congress, denying Congress its power as granted under the Constitution, and nine counts pertaining to violation of the Tenure of Office Act, which stated he could not dismiss any appointed official without the approval of Congress, even those he had appointed himself.[9] His administration was plagued by the struggles of Reconstruction and the lingering bitterness between North and South. His defense rested on the argument that such a law was unconstitutional, as the president must have the sole right to remove his subordinates because he is ultimately responsible for their actions.[10] Indeed, the framers considered this a responsibility of the presidential office. As James Wilson, who would become one of the first Supreme Court justices, said during his state's ratification of the Constitution: "We have a responsibility in the person of our President; he cannot act improperly, and hide either his negligence or inattention; he cannot roll upon any other person the weight of his criminality; no appointment can take place without his nomination; and he is responsible for every nomination he makes."[11] Johnson was acquitted by a single vote in the Senate and went on to finish his term. The Tenure of Office Act was repealed in 1887, and it was declared unconstitutional in 1926.

More than 130 years later, President William Jefferson Clinton was tried on two articles of impeachment, perjury and obstruction of justice. The charges stemmed from a long, complex inquiry into the president's past financial dealings and eventually arose from testimony Clinton gave during this inquiry about his involvement in extramarital affairs. In the hearings to decide if the Judicial Committee should start formal impeachment inquiry against Clinton, Wisconsin Representative F. James Sensenbrenner Jr. said: "What's at stake here is the rule of law. Even the president of the United States has no right to break the law. If the House votes down this inquiry… nothing will happen. The result will be a return to the imperial presidency of the Nixon era, where the White House felt that the laws did not apply to them, since they never would be punished. That would be a national tragedy of immense consequences."[12]

Clinton was ultimately acquitted of both charges after a 12-day trial. "We fulfilled our oath of office to discharge our duty according to the Constitution and when elected officials do that, democracy works," said Henry Hyde, chief prosecutor against the president.[13] Clinton apologized in a speech to the American public and served the remainder of his term.

Also politically relevant is the near-impeachment of President Richard Milhouse Nixon. The House Judiciary Committee passed three articles of impeachment against Nixon in 1974. Nixon resigned before the House could vote to impeach him, but had the House voted in favor of impeachment, the charges he would have faced included obstructing justice as it pertained to the Watergate break-ins, engaging "in conduct violating the constitutional rights of citizens," refusing to provide documents to the Judiciary Committee without providing a legal reason, and "assuming to himself the functions and judgments given to the House of Representatives by the Constitution."[14]

"One of the important lessons of Watergate was that unless the government trusts the people and conducts itself in an honorable fashion, then the people won't trust the government," said Archibald Cox, Watergate special prosecutor. "The long-range aim of the Watergate investigation and prosecution was to show that the government could cleanse itself and be put in a shape that the people could trust."[15]

While the framers intended impeachment as a tool to keep the executive branch in check, it applies not only to presidents and vice presidents but also to all "civil officers." The first American impeachment was against a senator from Tennessee, William Blount. In July 1797, the House of Representatives voted to impeach Senator Blount, who had been caught by President John Adams's administration plotting to conquer Spanish Florida and Louisiana for the British. When this scandal was made public, the Senate voted to expel him. The Senate dropped the impeachment charges a year later, citing lack of jurisdiction. Because of this precedent, it has since been commonly interpreted that neither senators nor representatives are subject to impeachment, though they do have their own internal disciplinary measures.[16]

Since 1789, there have been 17 impeachments by the House, 14 of which were tried in the Senate. Three were dismissed before they could come to trial. Included in these 17 formal cases are two presidents, one senator, one secretary of war, one Supreme Court justice, and 12 federal judges. Of this illustrious group, only seven federal judges have been convicted of wrongdoing and removed from office; the rest were acquitted.[17] The judges' crimes ranged from tax evasion and bribery to incitement to revolt and drunkenness. The most recent impeachment of a judge occurred in 1986, when Walter Nixon from Mississippi was impeached for lying to a grand jury. He was convicted and removed from office.[18]

"It would be the best way therefore to provide in the Constitution for the regular punishment of the Executive where his misconduct should deserve it," said Benjamin Franklin during the debates at the Constitutional Convention. "And for his honorable acquittal when he should be unjustly accused."[19] Whether it results in conviction or acquittal, ultimately, the value of impeachment is in the process. The framers understood this value intrinsically, and its worth is still evident today.

---

1   James Madison, "The Debates in the Federal Convention of 1787, reported by James Madison, July 20." Archived online at The Avalon Project, Yale Law School:
    www.yale.edu/lawweb/avalon/debates/720.htm

2   Impeachment Inquiry Staff, Committee on the Judiciary of the U.S. House of Representatives, *Constitutional Grounds for Presidential Impeachment* (Washington, D.C.: Public Affairs Press, 1974). Available online at www.washingtonpost.com/wp--srv/poliitics/special/clinton/stories/watergatedoc.hm

3   See the Senate's website, "Impeachment: Constitutional Origins":
    www.senate.gov/artandhistory/history/common/briefing/Senate_Impeac
    hment_Role.htm

4   Madison, "The Debates in the Federal Convention of 1787."

5   Madison, "The Debates in the Federal Convention of 1787."

6   Madison, "The Debates in the Federal Convention of 1787."

7   Committee on the Judiciary of the U.S. House, *Constitutional Grounds.*

8   Alexander Hamilton, *The Federalist Papers No. 65.* Archived online at
    The Avalon Project, Yale Law School:
    www.yale.edu/lawweb/avalon/federal/fed65.htm

9   The Articles of Impeachment against Andrew Johnson are included in
    the Appendix to this volume.

10 See www.historyplace.com/unitedstates/impeachments/johnson.htm.

11 Committee on the Judiciary of the U.S. House, *Constitutional Grounds.*

12 *Washington Post*, "Follow the Truth Wherever It Leads," October 9,
    1998. Available online at www.washingtonpost.com/wp-rv/politics/spe-
    cial/clinton/stories/text100998.htm

13 CNN & The Associated Press, "Clinton Acquitted; President Apologizes
    Again," February 12, 1999. Available online at www.cnn.com/ALLPOLI-
    TICS/stories/1999/02/12/impeachment/

14 The Articles of Impeachment against Richard M. Nixon are included in
    the Appendix to this volume.

15 As quoted in Bart Barnes, "Archibald Cox, 1912-2004: Watergate
    Prosecutor Faced Down the President," *The Washington Post*, May 30,
    2004. Available online at www.washingtonpost.com/wp-
    dyn/articles/A1755-2004May29.html

16 See Borgna Brunner, "A Short History of Impeachment":
    www.infoplease.com/spot/impeach.html.

17 U.S. Senate, "Impeachment: The Senate's Impeachment Role."

18 U.S. Senate, "Impeachment: The Senate's Impeachment Role."

19 Madison, "The Debates in the Federal Convention of 1787."

ARTICLES OF IMPEACHMENT EXHIBITED AGAINST ANDREW JOHNSON (1868)

Articles exhibited by the House of Representatives of the United States, in the name of themselves and all the people of the United States, against Andrew Johnson, President of the United States, in maintenance and support of their impeachment against him for high crimes and misdemeanors.

ARTICLE I.

That said Andrew Johnson, President of the United States, on the 21st day of February, in the year of our Lord, 1868, at Washington, in the District of Columbia, unmindful of the high duties of his office, of his oath of office, and of the requirement of the Constitution that he should take care that the laws be faithfully executed, did unlawfully and in violation of the Constitution and laws of the United States issue and order in writing for the removal of Edwin M. Stanton from the office of Secretary for the Department of War, said Edwin M. Stanton having been theretofore duly appointed and commissioned, by and with the advice and consent of the Senate of the United States, as such Secretary, and said Andrew Johnson, President of the United States, on the 12th day of August, in the year of our Lord 1867, and during the recess of said Senate, having been suspended by his order Edwin M. Stanton from said office, and within twenty days after the first day of the next meeting of said Senate, that is to say, on the 12th day of December, in the year last aforesaid, having reported to said Senate such suspension, with the evidence and reasons for his action in the case and the name of the person designated to perform the duties of such office temporarily until the next meeting of the Senate, and said Senate thereafterward, on the 13th day of January, in the year of our Lord 1868, having duly considered the evidence and reasons reported by said Andrew Johnson for said suspension, and having been refused to concur in said suspension, whereby and by force of the provisions of an act entitled "An act regulating the tenure of certain civil offices," passed March 2, 1867, said Edwin M. Stanton did forthwith resume the functions of his office, whereof the said Andrew Johnson had then and there due notice, and said Edwin Stanton, by reason of the premises, on said 21st day of February, being lawfully entitled to hold said office of Secretary for the Department of War, which said order for the removal of said Edwin M. Stanton is, in substance, as follows, that is to say:

EXECUTIVE MANSION,

WASHINGTON, D.C., *February* 21, 1868

Hon. E. M. Stanton, Secretary of War

SIR: By virtue of the power and authority vested in me, as President by the Constitution and laws of the United States, you are hereby removed from the office of Secretary for the Department of War, and your functions as such will terminate upon receipt of their communication. You will transfer to Brevet Major-General L. Thomas, Adjutant-General of the Army, who has this day been authorized and empowered to act as Secretary of War ad interim, all books, paper and other public property now in your custody and charge.

Respectfully yours,

ANDREW JOHNSON.

Which order was unlawfully issued, and with intent then are there to violate the act entitled "An act regulating the tenure of certain civil office," passed March 2, 1867; and, with the further intent contrary to the provisions of said act, and in violation thereof, and contrary to the provisions of the Constitution of the United States, and without the advice and consent of the Senate of the United States, the said Senate then and there being in session, to remove said Edwin M. Stanton from the office of Secretary for the Department of War, the said Edwin M. Stanton being then and there Secretary of War, and being then and there in the due and lawful execution of the duties of said office, whereby said Andrew Johnson, President of the United States, did then and there commit, and was guilty of a high misdemeanor in office.

ARTICLE II.

That on the 21st day of February, in the year of our Lord 1868, at Washington, in the District of Columbia, said Andrew Johnson, President of the United States, unmindful of the high duties of his office, of his oath of office, and in violation of the Constitution of the United States, and contrary to the provisions of an act entitled "An act regulating the tenure of certain civil offices," passed March 2, 1867, without the advice and consent of the Senate of the United States, said Senate then and there being in session, and without authority of law, did, with intent to violate the Constitution of the United States and the act aforesaid, issue and deliver to one Lorenzo Thomas a letter of authority, in substance as follows, that is to say:

EXECUTIVE MANSION,
WASHINGTON, D.C., *February* 21, 1868
To Brevet Major-General Lorenzo Thomas,

Adjutant General United States Army, Washington, D.C.

SIR: The Hon. Edwin M. Stanton having been this day removed from office as Secretary for the Department of War, you are hereby authorized and empowered to act as Secretary of War *ad interim,* and will immediately enter upon the discharge of the duties pertaining to that office.

Mr. Stanton has been instructed to transfer to you all the records, books, papers and other public property now in his custody and charge.

Respectfully yours,

ANDREW JOHNSON

then and there being no vacancy in said office of Secretary for the Department of War: whereby said Andrew Johnson, President of the United States, did then and there commit, and was guilty of a high misdemeanor in office.

ARTICLE III.

That said Andrew Johnson, President of the United States, on the 21st day of February, in the year of our Lord 1868, at Washington in the District of Columbia, did commit, and was guilty of a high misdemeanor in office, in this, that, without authority of law, while the Senate of the United States was then and there in session, he did appoint one Lorenzo Thomas to be Secretary for the Department of War, *ad interim,* without the advice and consent of the Senate, and with intent to violate the Constitution of the United States, no vacancy having happened in said office of Secretary for the Department of War during the recess of the Senate, and no vacancy existing in said office at the time, and which said appointment so made by Andrew Johnson, of said Lorenzo Thomas is in substance as follows, that is to say:

EXECUTIVE MANSION,

WASHINGTON, D.C., *February* 21, 1868

To Brevet Major-General Lorenzo Thomas,

Adjutant General United States Army, Washington, D.C.

SIR: The Hon. Edwin M. Stanton having been this day removed from office as Secretary for the Department of War, you are hereby authorized and empowered to act as Secretary of War *ad interim,* and will immediately enter upon the discharge of the duties pertaining to that office.

Mr. Stanton has been instructed to transfer to you all the records, books, papers and other public property now in his custody and charge.

Respectfully yours,

ANDREW JOHNSON

ARTICLE IV.

That said Andrew Johnson, President of the United States, unmindful of the high duties of his office, and of his oath of office, in violation of the Constitution and laws of the United States, on the 21st day of February, in the year of our Lord 1868, at Washington, in the District of Columbia, did unlawfully conspire with one Lorenzo Thomas, and with other persons to the House of Representatives unknown, with intent by intimidation and threats unlawfully to hinder and prevent Edwin M. Stanton, then and there, the Secretary for the Department of War, duly appointed under the laws of the United States, from holding said office of Secretary for the Department of War, contrary to and in violation of the Constitution of the United States, and of the provisions of an act entitled "An act to define and punish certain conspiracies," approved July 31, 1861, whereby said Andrew Johnson, President of the United States, did then and there commit and was guilty of high crime in office.

ARTICLE V.

That said Andrew Johnson, President of the United States, unmindful of the high duties of his office and of his oath of office, on the 21st of February, in the year of our Lord 1868, and on divers others days and time in said year before the 2nd day of March, A.D. 1868, at Washington, in the District of Columbia, did unlawfully conspire with one Lorenzo Thomas, and with other persons in the House of Representatives unknown, to prevent and hinder the execution of an act entitled "An act regulating the tenure of certain civil office," passed March 2, 1867, and in pursuance of said conspiracy, did attempt to prevent Edwin M. Stanton, then and there being Secretary for the Department of War, duly appointed and commissioned under the laws of the United States, from holding said office, whereby the said Andrew Johnson, President of the United States, did then and there commit and was guilty of high misdemeanor in office.

ARTICLE VI.

That said Andrew Johnson, President of the United States, unmindful of the high duties of his office and of his oath of office, on the 21st day of February, in the year of our Lord 1868, at Washington, in the District of Columbia, did unlawfully conspire with one Lorenzo Thomas, by force to seize, take, and possess the property of the United Sates in the Department of War, and then and there in the custody and charge of Edwin M. Stanton, Secretary for said Department, contrary to the provisions of an act entitled "An act to define and punish certain conspiracies," approved July 31, 1861, and with intent to violate and disregard an act entitled "An act regulating the tenure of certain civil offices," passed March 2, 1867, whereby said Andrew Johnson, President of the United States, did then and there commit a high crime in office.

ARTICLE VII.

That said Andrew Johnson, President of the United States, unmindful of the high duties of his office, and of his oath of office, on the 21st day of February, in the year of our Lord 1868, at Washington, in the District of Columbia, did unlawfully conspire with one Lorenzo Thomas with intent unlawfully to seize, take, and possess the property of the United States in the Department of War, in the custody and charge of Edwin M. Stanton, Secretary of said Department, with intent to violate and disregard the act entitled "An act regulating the tenure of certain civil offices," passed March 2, 1867, whereby said Andrew Johnson, President of the United States, did then and there commit a high misdemeanor in office.

ARTICLE VIII.

That said Andrew Johnson, President of the United States, unmindful of the high duties of his office and of his oath of office, with intent unlawfully to control the disbursements of the moneys appropriated for the military service and for the Department of War, on the 21st day of February, in the year of our Lord 1868, at Washington, in the District of Columbia, did unlawfully and contrary to the provisions of an act entitled "An act regulating the tenure of certain civil offices," passed March 2, 1867, and in violation of the Constitution of the United States, and without the advice and consent of the Senate of the United States, and while the Senate was then and there in session, there being no vacancy in the office of Secretary for the Department of War, with intent to violate and disregard the act aforesaid, then and there issue and deliver to one Lorenzo Thomas a letter of authority in writing, in substance as follows, that is to say:

EXECUTIVE MANSION,
WASHINGTON, D.C., *February* 21, 1868

To Brevet Major-General Lorenzo Thomas,
Adjutant General United States Army, Washington, D.C.
SIR: The Hon. Edwin M. Stanton having been this day removed from office as Secretary for the Department of War, you are hereby authorized and empowered to act as Secretary of War *ad interim*, and will immediately enter upon the discharge of the duties pertaining to that office.

Mr. Stanton has been instructed to transfer to you all the records, books, papers and other public property now in his custody and charge.

Respectfully yours,
ANDREW JOHNSON

Whereby said Andrew Johnson, President of the United States, did then and there commit and was guilty of a high misdemeanor in office.

ARTICLE IX.

That said Andrew Johnson, President of the United States, on the 22nd day of February, in the year of our Lord 1868, at Washington, in the District of Columbia, in disregard of the Constitution and the laws of the United States, duly enacted, as Commander-in-Chief of the Army of the United States, did bring before himself, then and there William H. Emory, a Major-General by brevet in the Army of the United States, actually in command of the department of Washington, and the military forces thereof, and did and there, as such Commander-in-Chief, declare to, and instruct said Emory, that part of a law of the United States, passed March 2, 1867, entitled "An act for making appropriations for the support of the Army for the year ending June 30, 1868, and for other purposes," especially the second section thereof, which provides, among other things, that "all orders and instructions relating to military operations issued by the President or Secretary of War, shall be issued through the General of the Army, and, in case of his inability, through the next in rank," was unconstitutional, and in contravention of the commission of said Emory, and which said provision of law had been theretofore duly and legally promulgated by general order for the government and direction of the Army of the United States, as the said Andrew Johnson then and there well knew, with intent thereby to induce said Emory, in his official capacity as Commander of the department of Washington, to violate the provisions of said act, and to take and receive, act upon and obey such orders as he, the said Andrew Johnson, might make and give, and which should not be issued through the General of the Army of the United States, according to the provisions of said act, and with the further intent thereby to enable him, the said Andrew Johnson, to prevent the execution of an act entitled "An act regulating the tenure of certain civil offices," passed March 2, 1867, and to unlawfully prevent Edwin M. Stanton, then being Secretary for the Department of War, from holding said office and discharging the duties thereof, whereby said Andrew Johnson, President of the United States, did then and there commit, and was guilty of a high misdemeanor in office.

ARTICLE X.

That said Andrew Johnson, President of the United States, unmindful of the high duties of his office and the dignity and proprieties thereof, and of the harmony and courtesies which ought to exist and be maintained between the executive and legislative branches of the Government of the United States, designing and intending to set aside the rightful authorities and powers of Congress, did attempt to bring into disgrace, ridicule, hatred, contempt and reproach the Congress of the United States, and the several branches thereof, to impair and destroy the regard and respect of all the good people of the United States for the Congress and legislative power thereof, (which all officers of the government ought inviolably to preserve and maintain) and to excite the odium and resentment of all good people of the United States against Congress and the laws by it duly and constitutionally enacted; and in pursuance of his said design and intent, openly and publicly and before divers assemblages of citizens of the United States, convened in divers parts thereof, to meet and receive said Andrew Johnson as the Chief Magistrate of the United States, did, on the 18th day of August, in the year of our Lord 1866, and on divers other days and times, as well before as afterward, make and declare, with a loud voice certain intemperate, inflammatory, and scandalous harangues, and therein utter loud threats and bitter menaces, as well against Congress as the laws of the United States duly enacted thereby, amid the cries, jeers and laughter of the multitudes then assembled in hearing, which are set forth in the several specifications hereinafter written, in substance and effect, that it to say:

SPECIFICATION FIRST. In this, that at Washington, in the District of Columbia, in the Executive Mansion, to a committee of citizens who called upon the President of the United States, speaking of and concerning the Congress of the United States, heretofore, to wit: On the 18th day of August, in the year of our Lord, 1866, in a loud voice, declare in substance and effect, among other things, that is to say:

"So far as the Executive Department of the government is concerned, the effort has been made to restore the Union, to heal the breach, to pour oil into the wounds which were consequent upon the struggle, and, to speak in a common phrase, to prepare, as the learned and wise physician would, a plaster healing in character and co-extensive with the wound. We thought and we think that we had partially succeeded, but as the work progresses, as reconstruction seemed to be taking place, and the country was becoming reunited, we found a disturbing and moving element opposing it. In alluding to that element it shall go no further than your Convention, and the distinguished gentleman who has delivered the report of the proceedings, I shall make no reference that I do not believe, and the time and the occasion justify.

"We have witnessed in one department of the government every endeavor to prevent the restoration of peace, harmony and union. We have seen hanging upon the verge of the government, as it were, a body called or which assumes to be the Congress of the United States, while in fact it is a Congress of only part of the States. We have seen this Congress pretend to be for the Union, when its every step and act tended to perpetuate disunion and make a disruption of States inevitable.

"We have seen Congress gradually encroach, step by step, upon consti-tutional rights, and violate day after day, and month after month, funda-mental principles of the government. We have seen a Congress that seemed to forget that there was a limit to the sphere and scope of legislation. We have seen a Congress in a minority assume to exercise power which, if allowed to be consummated, would result in despotism or monarchy itself."

SPECIFICATION SECOND. In this, that at Cleveland, in the State of Ohio, heretofore to wit: On the third day of September, in the year of our Lord, 1866, before a public assemblage of citizens and others, said Andrew Johnson, President of the United States, speaking of and concerning the Congress of the United States, did, in a loud voice, declare in substance and effect, among other things, that is to say:

"I will tell you what I did do? I called upon your Congress that is trying to break up the Government."

"In conclusion, beside that Congress had taken much pains to poison the constituents against him, what has Congress done? Have they done anything to restore the union of the States? No: On the contrary, they had done everything to prevent it: and because he stood now where he did when the rebellion commenced, he had been denounced as a traitor. Who had run greater risks or made greater sacrifices than himself? But Congress, factions and domineering, had undertaken to poison the minds of the American people."

SPECIFICATION THIRD. In this case, that at St. Louis, in the State of Missouri, heretofore to wit: On the 8th day of September, in the year of our Lord 1866, before a public assemblage of citizens and others, said Andrew Johnson, President of the United States, speaking of acts concerning the Congress of the United States, did, in a loud voice, declare in substance and effect, among other things, that is to say:

"Go on, perhaps if you had a word or two on the subject of New Orleans you might understand more about it than you do, and if you will go back and ascertain the cause of the riot at New Orleans, perhaps you will not be so prompt in calling out "New Orleans." If you will take up the riot of New Orleans and trace it back to its source and its immediate cause, you will find out who was responsible for the blood that was shed there. If you will take up the riot at New Orleans and trace it back to the Radical Congress, you will find that the riot at New Orleans was substantially planned. If you will take up the proceedings in their caucuses you will understand that they knew that a convention was to be called which was extinct by its powers having expired; that it was said that the intention was that a new government was to be organized, and on the organization of that government the intention was to enfranchise one portion of the population, called the colored population, and who had been emancipated, and at the same time disfranchise white men. When you design to talk about New Orleans you ought to understand what you are talking about. When you read the speeches that were made, and take up the facts on the Friday and Saturday before that convention sat, you will find that speeches were made incendiary in their character, exciting that portion of the population? the black population? to arm themselves and prepare for the shedding of blood. You will also find that convention did assemble in violation of law, and the intention of that convention was to supersede the organized authorities in the State of Louisiana, which had been organized by the government of the United States, and every man engaged in that rebellion, in the convention, with the intention of superseding and upturning the civil government which had been recognized by the Government of the United States, I say that he was a traitor to the Constitution of the United States, and hence you find that another rebellion was commenced, having its origin in the Radical Congress.

"So much for the New Orleans riot. And there was the cause and the origin of the blood that was shed, and every drop of blood that was shed is upon their skirts and they are responsible. I could test this thing a little closer, but will not do it here to-night. But when you talk about the causes and consequences that resulted from proceedings of that kind, perhaps, as I have been introduced here and you have provoked questions of this kind, though it does not provoke me, I will tell you a few wholesome things that have been done by this Radical Congress in connection with New Orleans and the extension of the elective franchise.

"I know that I have been traduced and abused. I know it has come in advance of me here, as elsewhere, that I have attempted to exercise an arbitrary power in resisting laws that were intended to be forced upon the government; that I had exercised that power; that I had abandoned the party that elected me, and that I was a traitor, because I exercised the veto power in attempting, and did arrest for a time, that which was called a "Freedmen's Bureau" bill. Yes, that I was a traitor. And I have been traduced; I have been slandered; I have been maligned; I have been called Judas Iscariot, and all that. Now, my countrymen, here to-night, it is very easy to indulge in epithets; it is easy to call a man a Judas, and cry out traitor, but when he is called upon to give arguments and facts he is very often found wanting. Judas Iscariot? Judas! There was a Judas, and he was one of the twelve Apostles. O, yes, the twelve Apostles had a Christ, and he never could have had a Judas unless he had twelve Apostles. If I have played the Judas who has been my Christ that I have played the Judas with? Was it Thad Stevens? Was it Wendell Phillips? Was it Charles Sumner? They are the men that stop and compare themselves with the Savior, and everybody that differs with them in opinion, and tries to stay and arrest their diabolical and nefarious policy is to be denounced as a Judas."

"Well, let me say to you, if you will stand by me in this action, if you will stand by me in trying to give the people a fair chance? soldiers and citizens? to participate in these office, God be willing, I will kick them out. I will kick them out just as fast as I can.

"Let me say to you, in concluding, that what I have said is what I intended to say; I was not provoked into this, and care not for their menaces, the taunts and the jeers. I care not for threats, I do not intend to be bullied by enemies, nor erawed by my friends. But, God willing, with your help, I will veto their measures whenever any of them come to me."

Which said utterances, declarations, threats and harangues, highly censurable in any, are peculiarly indecent and unbecoming in the Chief Magistrate of the United States, by means whereof the said Andrew Johnson has brought the high office of the President of the United States into contempt, ridicule and disgrace, to the great scandal of all good citizens, whereby said Andrew Johnson, President of the United States, did commit, and was then and there guilty of a high misdemeanor in office.

ARTICLE XI.

That the said Andrew Johnson, President of the United States, unmindful of the high duties of his office and of his oath of office, and in disregard of the Constitution and laws of the United States, did, heretofore, to wit: On the 18th day of August, 1866, at the city of Washington, and in the

District of Columbia, by public speech, declare and affirm in substance, that the Thirty-Ninth Congress of the United States was not a Congress of the United States authorized by the Constitution to exercise legislative power under the same; but, on the contrary, was a Congress of only part of the States, thereby denying and intending to deny, that the legislation of said Congress was valid or obligatory upon him, the said Andrew Johnson, except in so far as he saw fit to approve the same, and also thereby denying the power of the said Thirty-Ninth Congress to propose amendments to the Constitution of the United States. And in pursuance of said declaration, the said Andrew Johnson, President of the United States, afterwards, to wit: On the 21st day of February, 1868, at the city of Washington, D.C., did, unlawfully and in disregard of the requirements of the Constitution that he should take care that the laws be faithfully executed, attempt to prevent the execution of an act entitled "An act regulating the tenure of certain civil office," passed March 2, 1867, by unlawfully devising and contriving and attempting to devise and contrive means by which he should prevent Edwin M. Stanton from forthwith resuming the functions of the office of Secretary for the Department of War, notwithstanding the refusal of the Senate to concur in the suspension therefore made by the said Andrew Johnson of said Edwin M. Stanton from said office of Secretary for the Department of War; and also by further unlawfully devising and contriving, and attempting to devise and contrive, means then and there to prevent the execution of an act entitled "An act making appropriations for the support of the Army for the fiscal year ending June 30,1868, and for other purposes," approved March 2, 1867. And also to prevent the execution of an act entitled "An act to provide for the more efficient government of the rebel States," passed March 2, 1867. Whereby the said Andrew Johnson, President of the United States, did then, to wit: on the 21st day of February, 1868, at the city of Washington, commit and was guilty of a high misdemeanor in office.

ARTICLES OF IMPEACHMENT AGAINST RICHARD M. NIXON ADOPTED BY THE COMMITTEE ON THE JUDICIARY (JULY 27, 1974)

RESOLVED, *That Richard M. Nixon, President of the United States, is impeached for high crimes and misdemeanours, and that the following articles of impeachment to be exhibited to the Senate:*

ARTICLES OF IMPEACHMENT EXHIBITED BY THE HOUSE OF REPRESEN-TATIVES OF THE UNITED STATES OF AMERICA IN THE NAME OF ITSELF AND OF ALL OF THE PEOPLE OF THE UNITED STATES OF AMERICA, AGAINST RICHARD M. NIXON, PRESIDENT OF THE UNITED STATES OF AMERICA, IN MAINTENANCE AND SUPPORT OF ITS IMPEACHMENT AGAINST HIM FOR HIGH CRIMES AND MISDEMEANOURS.

ARTICLE I.

In his conduct of the office of President of the United States, Richard M. Nixon, in violation of his constitutional oath faithfully to execute the office of President of the United States and, to the best of his ability, preserve, protect, and defend the Constitution of the United States, and in violation of his constitutional duty to take care that the laws be faithfully executed, has prevented, obstructed, and impeded the administration of justice, in that:

On June 17, 1972, and prior thereto, agents of the Committee for the Re-election of the President committed unlawful entry of the headquarters of the Democratic National Committee in Washington, District of Columbia, for the purpose of securing political intelligence. Subsequent thereto, Richard M. Nixon, using the powers of his high office, engaged personally and through his close subordinates and agents, in a course of conduct or plan designed to delay, impede, and obstruct the investigation of such illegal entry; to cover up, conceal and protect those responsible; and to conceal the existence and scope of other unlawful covert activities.

The means used to implement this course of conduct or plan included one or more of the following:

(1) making false or misleading statements to lawfully authorized investigative officers and employees of the United States;

(2) withholding relevant and material evidence or information from lawfully authorized investigative officers and employees of the United States;

(3) approving, condoning, acquiescing in, and counselling witnesses with respect to the giving of false or misleading statements to lawfully authorized investigative officers and employees of the United States and false or misleading testimony in duly instituted judicial and congressional proceedings;

(4) interfering or endeavouring to interfere with the conduct of investigations by the Department of Justice of the United States, the Federal Bureau of Investigation, the office of Watergate Special Prosecution Force, and Congressional Committees;

(5) approving, condoning, and acquiescing in, the surreptitious payment of substantial sums of money for the purpose of obtaining the silence or influencing the testimony of witnesses, potential witnesses or individuals who participated in such unlawful entry and other illegal activities;

(6) endeavouring to misuse the Central Intelligence Agency, an agency of the United States;

(7) disseminating information received from officers of the Department of Justice of the United States to subjects of investigations conducted by lawfully authorized investigative officers and employees of the United States, for the purpose of aiding and assisting such subjects in their attempts to avoid criminal liability;

(8) making or causing to be made false or misleading public statements for the purpose of deceiving the people of the United States into believing that a thorough and complete investigation had been conducted with respect to allegations of misconduct on the part of personnel of the executive branch of the United States and personnel of the Committee for the Re-election of the President, and that there was no involvement of such personnel in such misconduct: or

(9) endeavouring to cause prospective defendants, and individuals duly tried and convicted, to expect favoured treatment and consideration in return for their silence or false testimony, or rewarding individuals for their silence or false testimony.

In all of this, Richard M. Nixon has acted in a manner contrary to his trust as President and subversive of constitutional government, to the great prejudice of the cause of law and justice and to the manifest injury of the people of the United States.

Wherefore Richard M. Nixon, by such conduct, warrants impeachment and trial, and removal from office.

ADOPTED 27-11 by the Committee on the Judiciary of the House of Representatives, at 7.07pm on Saturday, 27th July, 1974, in Room 2141 of the Rayburn Office Building, Washington D.C.

ARTICLE II.

Using the powers of the office of President of the United States, Richard M. Nixon, in violation of his constitutional oath faithfully to execute the office of President of the United States and, to the best of his ability, preserve, protect, and defend the Constitution of the United States, and in disregard of his constitutional duty to take care that the laws be faithfully executed, has repeatedly engaged in conduct violating the constitutional rights of citizens, impairing the due and proper administration of justice and the conduct of lawful inquiries, or contravening the laws governing agencies of the executive branch and the purposed of these agencies.

This conduct has included one or more of the following:

(1) He has, acting personally and through his subordinates and agents, endeavoured to obtain from the Internal Revenue Service, in violation of the constitutional rights of citizens, confidential information contained in income tax returns for purposed not authorized by law, and to cause, in violation of the constitutional rights of citizens, income tax audits or other income tax investigations to be initiated or conducted in a discriminatory manner.

(2) He misused the Federal Bureau of Investigation, the Secret Service, and other executive personnel, in violation or disregard of the constitutional rights of citizens, by directing or authorizing such agencies or personnel to conduct or continue electronic surveillance or other investigations for purposes unrelated to national security, the enforcement of laws, or any other lawful function of his office; he did direct, authorize, or permit the use of information obtained thereby for purposes unrelated to national security, the enforcement of laws, or any other lawful function of his office; and he did direct the concealment of certain records made by the Federal Bureau of Investigation of electronic surveillance.

(3) He has, acting personally and through his subordinates and agents, in violation or disregard of the constitutional rights of citizens, authorized and permitted to be maintained a secret investigative unit within the office of the President, financed in part with money derived from campaign contributions, which unlawfully utilized the resources of the Central Intelligence Agency, engaged in covert and unlawful activities, and attempted to prejudice the constitutional right of an accused to a fair trial.

(4) He has failed to take care that the laws were faithfully executed by failing to act when he knew or had reason to know that his close subordinates endeavoured to impede and frustrate lawful inquiries by duly constituted executive, judicial and legislative entities concerning the unlawful entry into the headquarters of the Democratic National Committee, and the cover-up thereof, and concerning other unlawful activities including those relating to the confirmation of Richard Kleindienst as Attorney General of the United States, the electronic surveillance of private citizens, the break-in into the offices of Dr. Lewis Fielding, and the campaign financing practices of the Committee to Re-elect the President.

(5) In disregard of the rule of law, he knowingly misused the executive power by interfering with agencies of the executive branch, including the Federal Bureau of Investigation, the Criminal Division, and the Office of Watergate Special Prosecution Force, of the Department of Justice, and the Central Intelligence Agency, in violation of his duty to take care that the laws be faithfully executed.

In all of this, Richard M. Nixon has acted in a manner contrary to his trust as President and subversive of constitutional government, to the great prejudice of the cause of law and justice and to the manifest injury of the people of the United States.

Wherefore Richard M. Nixon, by such conduct, warrants impeachment and trial, and removal from office.

ADOPTED 28-10 by the Committee on the Judiciary of the House of Representatives.

ARTICLE III.

In his conduct of the office of President of the United States, Richard M. Nixon, contrary to his oath faithfully to execute the office of President of the United States and, to the best of his ability, preserve, protect, and defend the Constitution of the United States, and in violation of his constitutional duty to take care that the laws be faithfully executed, has failed without lawful cause or excuse to produce papers and things as directed by duly authorized subpoenas issued by the Committee on the Judiciary of the House of Representatives on April 11, 1974, May 15, 1974, May 30, 1974, and June 24, 1974, and willfully disobeyed such subpoenas. The subpoenaed papers and things were deemed necessary by the Committee in order to resolve by direct evidence fundamental, factual questions relating to Presidential direction, knowledge or approval of actions demonstrated by other evidence to be substantial grounds for impeachment of the President. In refusing to produce these papers and things Richard M. Nixon, substituting his judgment as to what materials were necessary for the inquiry, interposed the powers of the Presidency against the lawful subpoenas of the House of Representatives, thereby assuming to himself functions and judgments necessary to the exercise of the sole power of impeachment vested by the Constitution in the House of Representatives.

In all of this, Richard M. Nixon has acted in a manner contrary to his trust as President and subversive of constitutional government, to the great prejudice of the cause of law and justice, and to the manifest injury of the people of the United States.

Wherefore Richard M. Nixon, by such conduct, warrants impeachment and trial, and removal from office.

ADOPTED 21-17 by the Committee on the Judiciary of the House of Representatives.

ARTICLES OF IMPEACHMENT AGAINST WILLIAM JEFFERSON CLINTON (1998)

RESOLVED, *That William Jefferson Clinton, President of the United States, is impeached for high crimes and misdemeanors, and that the following articles of impeachment be exhibited to the United States Senate:*

ARTICLES OF IMPEACHMENT EXHIBITED BY THE HOUSE OF REPRESENTATIVES OF THE UNITED STATES OF AMERICA IN THE NAME OF ITSELF AND OF THE PEOPLE OF THE UNITED STATES OF AMERICA, AGAINST WILLIAM JEFFERSON CLINTON, PRESIDENT OF THE UNITED STATES OF AMERICA, IN MAINTENANCE AND SUPPORT OF ITS IMPEACHMENT AGAINST HIM FOR HIGH CRIMES AND MISDEMEANORS.

ARTICLE I.

In his conduct while President of the United States, William Jefferson Clinton, in violation of his constitutional oath faithfully to execute the office of President of the United States and, to the best of his ability, preserve, protect, and defend the Constitution of the United States, and in violation of his constitutional duty to take care that the laws be faithfully executed, has willfully corrupted and manipulated the judicial process of the United States for his personal gain and exoneration, impeding the administration of justice, in that:

On August 17, 1998, William Jefferson Clinton swore to tell the truth, the whole truth, and nothing but the truth before a Federal grand jury of the United States. Contrary to that oath, William Jefferson Clinton willfully provided perjurious, false and misleading testimony to the grand jury concerning one or more of the following:

(1) the nature and details of his relationship with a subordinate Government employee;

(2) prior perjurious, false and misleading testimony he gave in a Federal civil rights action brought against him;

(3) prior false and misleading statements he allowed his attorney to make to a Federal judge in that civil rights action; and

(4) his corrupt efforts to influence the testimony of witnesses and to impede the discovery of evidence in that civil rights action.

In doing this, William Jefferson Clinton has undermined the integrity of his office, has brought disrepute on the Presidency, has betrayed his trust as President, and has acted in a manner subversive of the rule of law and justice, to the manifest injury of the people of the United States.

Wherefore, William Jefferson Clinton, by such conduct, warrants impeachment and trial, and removal from office and disqualification to hold and enjoy any office of honor, trust, or profit under the United States.

ARTICLE II.

In his conduct while President of the United States, William Jefferson Clinton, in violation of his constitutional oath faithfully to execute the office of President of the United States and, to the best of his ability, preserve, protect, and defend the Constitution of the United States, and in violation of his constitutional duty to take care that the laws be faithfully executed, has prevented, obstructed, and impeded the administration of justice, and has to that end engaged personally, and through his subordinates and agents, in a course of conduct or scheme designed to delay, impede, cover up, and conceal the existence of evidence and testimony related to a Federal civil rights action brought against him in a duly instituted judicial proceeding.

The means used to implement this course of conduct or scheme included one or more of the following acts:

(1) On or about December 17, 1997, William Jefferson Clinton corruptly encouraged a witness in a Federal civil rights action brought against him to execute a sworn affidavit in that proceeding that he knew to be perjurious, false and misleading.

(2) On or about December 17, 1997, William Jefferson Clinton corruptly encouraged a witness in a Federal civil rights action brought against him to give perjurious, false and misleading testimony if and when called to testify personally in that proceeding.

(3) On or about December 28, 1997, William Jefferson Clinton corruptly engaged in, encouraged, or supported a scheme to conceal evidence that had been subpoenaed in a Federal civil rights action brought against him.

(4) Beginning on or about December 7, 1997, and continuing through and including January 14, 1998, William Jefferson Clinton intensified and succeeded in an effort to secure job assistance to a witness in a Federal civil rights action brought against him in order to corruptly prevent the truthful testimony of that witness in that proceeding at a time when the truthful testimony of that witness would have been harmful to him.

(5) On January 17, 1998, at his deposition in a Federal civil rights action brought against him, William Jefferson Clinton corruptly allowed his attorney to make false and misleading statements to

a Federal judge characterizing an affidavit, in order to prevent questioning deemed relevant by the judge. Such false and misleading statements were subsequently acknowledged by his attorney in a communication to that judge.

(6) On or about January 18 and January 20-21, 1998, William Jefferson Clinton related a false and misleading account of events relevant to a Federal civil rights action brought against him to a potential witness in that proceeding, in order to corruptly influence the testimony of that witness.

(7) On or about January 21, 23, and 26, 1998, William Jefferson Clinton made false and misleading statements to potential witnesses in a Federal grand jury proceeding in order to corruptly influence the testimony of those witnesses. The false and misleading statements made by William Jefferson Clinton were repeated by the witnesses to the grand jury, causing the grand jury to receive false and misleading information.

In all of this, William Jefferson Clinton has undermined the integrity of his office, has brought disrepute on the Presidency, has betrayed his trust as President, and has acted in a manner subversive of the rule of law and justice, to the manifest injury of the people of the United States.

Wherefore, William Jefferson Clinton, by such conduct, warrants impeachment and trial, and removal from office and disqualification to hold and enjoy any office of honor, trust, or profit under the United States.

Passed the House of Representatives December 19, 1998.

NEWT GINGRICH, Speaker of the House of Representatives.
Attest: ROBIN H. CARLE, Clerk.

A NOTE ON PROCEDURE

Contrary to popular belief, "impeachment" does not refer to the conviction of a president and his or her eviction from office; it is the process whereby charges against the president—and other federal officials, such as judges, cabinet members, and the vice president, but not the members of either house of Congress—are prosecuted by members of the House of Representatives before the U.S. Senate. Nor does impeachment imply any criminal wrongdoing. Rather, impeachment is concerned with acts of political misconduct. As such, the sole penalty faced by those undergoing impeachment is removal from office and disqualification from further office. This removal does not exonerate an official from facing any further charges in a criminal court, however.

Three documents control the procedures of impeachment:

(1) the Constitution of the United States, which sets forth specific rules for the removal of the executive;

(2) the House Rules and Manual, specifically that portion known as "Jefferson's Manual of Parliamentary Practice," so called because it is based on a core handbook with references to English precedent that Thomas Jefferson composed for himself while presiding over the Senate;

(3) the Rules of Procedure and Practice in the Senate When Sitting on Impeachment Trials.

As set forth by the Constitution, the House of Representatives has the sole power to impeach, and the Senate has the sole power to try those so impeached. Conviction comes only upon a two thirds vote of the Senate, in a trial presided over by the chief justice of the Supreme Court.

As governed by Jefferson's Manual and the Constitution, impeachment can arise from charges brought forth in a number of ways. They can arise from the work of an investigatory committee, grand jury, or special prosecutor. They can also be brought forth by an individual on the floor of the House, or by the President him- or herself (against a judge or cabinet member, for example). Charges can also be brought by a state legislature. Citing a 1625 British resolution, Thomas Jefferson promulgated the idea that charges could be brought forth by those outside the halls of government via what was known as "common fame"—things that were widely known or reported upon in the press. As Jefferson put it, "Common fame is a good ground for the House to proceed by inquiry, and even to accusation."

Once a charge is determined by the House to be worthy of review, it is assigned to the House Judiciary Committee for examination of the evidence, a process that may include hearings. If the committee finds an official impeachment investigation is warranted, it must then ask the full House for permission to proceed. At the end of such an approved investigation, the Judiciary Committee decides whether to forward articles of impeachment to the full House. Articles thus presented to the House are subject to debate, following which a separate vote is taken on each article. A simple majority on any article is needed for the accused individual to be impeached. If a majority is thus attained, the House then appoints members to act as "managers," or prosecutors (these appointments are made by the Speaker of the House or by a majority vote). The "managers" then present the articles of impeachment to the secretary of the Senate for trial.

As dictated by the Senate Rules and the Constitution, in the case of impeachment of a president, the Senate trial is presided over by the chief justice, although any ruling by the chief justice can be overturned by a majority vote of the Senate. The Senate acts as a jury; the trial begins with the membership swearing an oath to "do impartial justice according to the Constitution." The accused may appear but is not forced to do so, and is allowed to be represented by counsel, and to present witnesses and evidence, as well as to cross-examine all witnesses brought forth by the prosecution.

The Constitution, finally, determines the end game: A two thirds vote of the Senate on any article is required for conviction, with conviction leading to permanent removal from office, as well as permanent disqualification from holding further public office.

ARTICLE I

U.S. Code, Title 50, Chapter 36:
Foreign Intelligence Surveillance Act (FISA)
www4.law.cornell.edu/uscode/html/uscode50/usc_sup
_01_50_10_36.html

The Foreign Intelligence Surveillance Act:
An Overview of the Statutory Framework and Recent
Judicial Decisions by the Congressional Research
Service, April 25, 2005
www.fas.org/sgp/crs/intel/RL30465.pdf

Department of Justice Letter on Legal Authority for
NSA Surveillance from Asst. Attorney General William
E. Moschella, December 22, 2005
www.fas.org/irp/agency/doj/fisa/doj122205.pdf

Presidential Authority to Conduct Warrantless
Electronic Surveillance to Gather Foreign Intelligence
Information by the Congressional Research Service,
January 5, 2006
www.fas.org/sgp/crs/intel/m010506.pdf

Statutory Procedures Under Which Congress Is To Be
Informed of U.S. Intelligence Activities, Including
Covert Actions by the Congressional Research
Service, January 18, 2006
www.fas.org/sgp/crs/intel/m011806.pdf

Legal Authorities Supporting the Activities of the
National Security Agency Described by the President
A White Paper by the Department of Justice,
January 19, 2006
www.fas.org/irp/nsa/doj011906.pdf

"Constitution in Crisis: Domestic Surveillance and
Executive Power" A Judiciary Democratic
Congressional Briefing, January 20, 2006
www.house.gov/judiciary_democrats/nsabrief.html

ARTICLE II

U.S. Intelligence and Policy Making: The Iraq
Experience by the Congressional Research Service,
December 2, 2005
fpc.state.gov/documents/organization/58268.pdf

UN Charter
www.un.org/aboutun/charter

Downing Street Memo, a site containing information
about the Downing Street Memo and numerous other
documents that relate to the Iraq War
www.downingstreetmemo.com

ARTICLE III

Texts of the Geneva Conventions of 1949 and 1977
and International Treaties on the Conduct of War
www.genevaconventions.org

Renditions: Constraints Imposed by Laws on Torture
by the Congressional Research Service,
September 22, 2005
www.fas.org/sgp/crs/natsec/RL32890.pdf

Bush Administration Memos on Torture
www.nytimes.com/ref/international/24MEMO-GUIDE.html

Guantanamo Detainees: Habeas Corpus Challenges in
Federal Court by the Congressional Research Service,
December 7, 2005
www.fas.org/sgp/crs/natsec/RL33180.pdf

ARTICLE IV

The Conyers Report also known as The Constitution
in Crisis; The Downing Street Minutes and Deception,
Manipulation, Torture, Retribution, and Coverups in
the Iraq War
www.house.gov/judiciary_democrats/iraqrept122005/ir
aqreptweb.htm

Impeachment History
www.pbs.org/newshour/impeachment/timeline

Impeachment Documents Relating to a U.S. President
www.lib.auburn.edu/madd/docs/impeach.html

House Rules and Manual,
including "Jefferson's Manual" and the Constitution
www.gpoaccess.gov/hrm/index.html

 **centerforconstitutionalrights**

This book is the work of the Center for Constitutional Rights and Melville House Publishing. Contributors include CCR President Michael Ratner; CCR Legal Director William Goodman; CCR attorneys Shayana Kadidal and Maria LaHood; CCR cooperating attorney Jaykumar Menon; and CCR Communications Coordinator Jen Nessel. Barbara Olshansky, Rachel Meeropol, Kelly McAnnany, Olivia Breese, and Adriana Piñón provided valuable assistance with the project.

The Center for Constitutional Rights is a non-profit legal and educational organization dedicated to advancing and protecting the rights guaranteed by the U.S. Constitution and the Universal Declaration of Human Rights. Founded in 1966 by attorneys who represented civil rights demonstrators in the South, CCR is committed to the creative use of law as a positive force for social change.

FOR MORE INFORMATION:

THE CENTER FOR CONSTITUTIONAL RIGHTS
666 BROADWAY, 7TH FLOOR
NEW YORK, NY 10012
(212) 614-6464
WWW.CCR-NY.ORG